DECEMBER

Sunday	Monday	Tuesday	Wednesday	Thursday	Friday	Saturday
			1	2	3	4
5	6	7	8	9	10	11
12	13	14	15	16	17	18
19	20	21	22	23	24 Christmas Eve	25 Christmas Day
26	27	28	29	30	31 New Year's Eve	

Christmas

with Southern Living

1999

Oxmoor House®

Christmas
with Southern Living
1999

Edited by Rebecca Brennan
and Whitney Wheeler Pickering

CONTENTS

ISBN: 0-8487-1869-0
ISSN: 0747-7791
Manufactured in the United States of America
First Printing 1999

Editor-in-Chief: Nancy Fitzpatrick Wyatt
Senior Copy/Homes Editor: Olivia Kindig Wells
Senior Food Editor: Susan Payne Stabler
Art Director: James Boone

Christmas with Southern Living 1999

Editor: Rebecca Brennan
Food Editor: Whitney Wheeler Pickering
Copy Editors: Keri Bradford Anderson, Cathy Ritter Scholl
Editorial Assistant: Lauren Caswell Brooks
Associate Art Director: Cynthia R. Cooper
Designer: Emily Albright Parrish
Senior Photographers: Jim Bathie, John O'Hagan
Photographer: Brit Huckabay
Senior Photo Stylist: Kay E. Clarke
Photo Stylists: Virginia R. Cravens, Linda Baltzell Wright
Illustrator: Kelly Davis
Director, Test Kitchens: Kathleen Royal Phillips
Assistant Director, Test Kitchens: Gayle Hays Sadler
Test Kitchens Staff: Julie Christopher; Natalie E. King;
L. Victoria Knowles; Jan A. Smith; Kate M. Wheeler, R.D.
Publishing Systems Administrator: Rick Tucker
Director, Production and Distribution: Phillip Lee
Associate Production Manager: James E. McDaniel
Production Assistant: Faye Porter Bonner

Season's Celebrations 6

Decorating for the Holidays 22

Holiday Fare 68

Gifts of the Season 124

Patterns 146
Sources 154

Index 156
Contributors 160

Season's Celebrations

'Tis the season to be jolly, and you will be with pages of inspiring ideas for decorations and a delicious make-ahead menu for the Christmas feast.

A FRESH APPROACH TO THE HOLIDAYS

Feathers, flowers, and plenty of fresh greenery create a contemporary holiday mood in this traditional home.

Behind the classic facade of Ed and Barbara Randle's historic home lies a vividly colored, often whimsical interior that reflects Barbara's free-spirited manner. When she asked good friend and interior designer Rick Stembridge to decorate her home for the Christmas season, he mixed unconventional and traditional elements to create a contemporary look that suited both the holidays and Barbara's eclectic style.

With Barbara's bright red and yellow walls in mind, Rick chose some up-to-the-minute variations of the traditional red and green, using tomato red and lime green accents throughout the house. He relied on fresh materials to fashion everything from garlands to tree decorations to the lavish dining table centerpiece. Fresh greenery and fruit at the entrance set a fragrant, festive mood that's carried through the entire house.

A garland of fresh greenery intertwined with strings of tiny white lights frames the entrance to the Hoover-Randle House located in Birmingham, Alabama. Cherubs and bows accent the garland.

Rick Stembridge spreads holiday cheer and creative interior designs to more than twenty-five homes in the weeks between Thanksgiving and Christmas.

Barbara Randle's holiday decorations complement her home's distinctive interior design.

Turn the page for Rick's secret to a sensational center-piece—one simple floral bouquet times seven.

A generously decorated and colorful tree nestles inside the graceful curve of the entry-way staircase. Tree trimmings include gold stars hung from gold ribbon, ball ornaments, velvet grapes in red and lime tones, feathers, clove-studded lemons, and yellow oncidium orchids. Rick gathered large gold ornaments to use as a tree topper and a newel post embellishment.

Green apples, a surprise accent for candlesticks on the foyer table, add a shot of bright color in the room. Ostrich feathers are tied to the candlesticks with gold-trimmed red ribbon.

Seven cylindrical vases (drinking glasses will work, too) filled with Bells-of-Ireland, yellow orchids, and red marjan roses (the same color as the walls) placed upon a length of lime green ribbon form a stunning dining table centerpiece. In keeping with the traditional style of Barbara's dining room, Rick added a classic touch, using magnolia leaves to fill in around the vases.

The reflected light from a gold-framed mirror sets off a fresh evergreen wreath accented with gold cherubs and a large bow. The wreath is secured with a length of ribbon looped over the top of the mirror. Evergreen clippings drape over the mantel and entwine with ribbons and twigs.

A small wreath draws attention to but doesn't overpower the glass front door. The wreath introduces
decorative elements that reappear throughout the home's interior—fresh greenery; ostrich feathers; red,
green, and gold ribbons; glass ball ornaments; cherubs; and clove-studded lemons.

MAKE-AHEAD CHRISTMAS MENU

This menu features foolproof dishes that you can assemble with minimal fuss, even when time is tight. Recipes include commercially prepared ingredients, and you can make many of the recipes ahead for last-minute assembly and baking. Relax and enjoy the holiday!

Peppered Beef Tenderloin (page 115)

Sweet Potatoes with Cranberry Sauce
(page 18)

Company Rice (page 18)

Glazed Onions (page 19)

Lemon Green Bean Bundles (page 20)

Stained Glass Salad (page 20)

Herbed Fan Tan Dinner Rolls (page 92)
or store-bought rolls

Bûche de Noël (page 109)
or Pumpkin Chess Pie (page 21)

Cabernet Sauvignon   Coffee

Make-Ahead Game Plan

A Week Ahead
• Prepare and freeze Herbed Fan Tan Dinner Rolls in paper-lined muffin cups. Underbake them by 2 minutes, cool completely, and seal in a freezer bag; freeze.

Three Days Ahead
• Purchase all ingredients.

Two Days Ahead
• Prepare and chill Stained Glass Salad.
• Prepare Bûche de Noël; store in an airtight container.
• Set and decorate table.

One Day Ahead
• Prepare and chill Sweet Potatoes with Cranberry Sauce, Lemon Green Bean Bundles, and Peppered Beef Tenderloin (do not bake tenderloin).
• Prepare, bake, and chill Glazed Onions. (If you have plenty of oven space, omit baking the onions prior to chilling; then bake them for 25 minutes prior to dinner rather than reheating them in the microwave.)

Christmas Day
Three Hours Ahead
• Prepare Company Rice in slow cooker.

Two Hours Ahead
• Unmold and garnish Stained Glass Salad.
• Thaw Herbed Fan Tan Dinner Rolls (in bag at room temperature).

One Hour Ahead
• Bake Peppered Beef Tenderloin.
• Remove sweet potatoes, Glazed Onions, and green beans from refrigerator; let stand at room temperature.

Thirty Minutes Ahead
• Bake Sweet Potatoes with Cranberry Sauce.

Fifteen Minutes Ahead
• Microwave Glazed Onions, if they need reheating.
• Heat Lemon Green Bean Bundles.
• Heat dinner rolls: return rolls to muffin pans; reheat at 350° for 6 to 8 minutes or until lightly browned.
• Pour wine, and make coffee.

Peppered Beef Tenderloin (page 115), Sweet Potatoes with Cranberry Sauce (page 18), Lemon Green Bean Bundles (page 20), and Company Rice (page 18)

SWEET POTATOES WITH CRANBERRY SAUCE

To save time, you can use frozen sweet potato patties (found in the meat or frozen foods freezer of your supermarket) in this recipe. The patties are fragile, but you may find the trade-off worth it if you're pinched for time.

4   pounds sweet potatoes (about 6 small)
1   (16-ounce) can whole-berry cranberry
        sauce
1   cup fresh cranberries
¾   cup orange juice
½   cup firmly packed brown sugar
2   tablespoons butter or margarine
¾   teaspoon ground cinnamon
¼   teaspoon ground nutmeg

Make-Ahead: Wash sweet potatoes; prick several times with a fork. Arrange on paper towels in microwave oven, leaving 1" between each. Microwave at HIGH 22 minutes, rearranging potatoes once; let stand 5 minutes. Cool potatoes to touch; peel and cut into ½" slices. Arrange slices in a slightly overlapping spiral pattern 1 to 2 layers thick in a 12" round baking dish; set aside.

   Meanwhile, combine cranberry sauce and remaining 6 ingredients in a saucepan; bring to a boil. Reduce heat; simmer, uncovered, 5 minutes. Pour cranberry mixture over sweet potatoes; cool. Cover tightly, and chill overnight.

When Ready to Serve: Remove from refrigerator; let stand 30 minutes. Uncover and bake at 350° for 30 minutes or until thoroughly heated and bubbly. **Yield:** 8 servings.

COMPANY RICE

Today's supermarkets carry a variety of wild rice blends. Pick one for a 5- to 15-minute substitute for Company Rice.

1   (6-ounce) package wild rice
¼   cup butter or margarine, cut into pieces
1   (8-ounce) package sliced fresh mushrooms
3   green onions, chopped (about ¼ cup)
½   teaspoon salt
1   (14½-ounce) can ready-to-serve chicken broth
2   tablespoons sherry
½   cup sliced almonds, toasted (optional)

Make-Ahead Slow Cooker Method: Combine first 7 ingredients in a 4-quart electric slow cooker; cover and cook on HIGH setting 3 hours. Drain excess liquid, if necessary. Fluff rice with a fork; sprinkle with almonds, if desired. **Yield:** 8 servings.

Cooktop Method: Melt butter in a 2-quart saucepan over medium heat. Stir in rice; cook, stirring occasionally, 5 minutes. Add mushrooms and next 4 ingredients; bring to a boil. Cover, reduce heat, and simmer 1 hour and 5 minutes or until rice is done; drain excess liquid, if desired. Fluff rice with a fork; sprinkle with almonds.

A ribbon and a sprig of fresh rosemary add a fragrant touch to handmade place cards.

GLAZED ONIONS

If you'd like, save time by purchasing frozen pearl onions and skipping the blanching process.

2   pounds white or red pearl onions, peeled (about 4
        cups)* or 1 (16-ounce) bag frozen pearl onions
⅓   cup butter or margarine
½   cup firmly packed brown sugar
⅓   cup light corn syrup
½   teaspoon salt
1   tablespoon chopped fresh parsley
        (optional)

Make-Ahead: Arrange onions in a steamer basket over boiling water; cover and steam 10 minutes or until tender. Place in a lightly greased 8" square baking dish.

Melt butter in a small saucepan over medium-low heat. Add sugar, syrup, and salt; bring to a boil over medium heat. Reduce heat; simmer 5 minutes. Pour over onions.

Cover and bake at 350° for 25 minutes. Remove from oven, and cool. Cover with aluminum foil, and chill overnight.

When Ready to Serve: Remove aluminum foil from baking dish; cover dish tightly with heavy-duty plastic wrap. Fold back a small edge (or corner) of wrap to allow steam to escape.

Microwave at MEDIUM (50% power) 12 minutes or until thoroughly heated, turning dish once. Sprinkle with parsley, if desired. **Yield:** 8 servings.

A quick and easy way to peel pearl onions is to trim bottom ends of onions and blanch onions in batches for about 45 seconds in rapidly boiling water. (It's important to blanch in batches so that the water remains at a boil.) Drain onions, and immediately place in a bowl of ice water to stop the cooking process. Simply squeeze trimmed end of each onion gently, and the skins will slide right off.

LEMON GREEN BEAN BUNDLES

The most obvious time-saver in this recipe is to omit the bundling. You can also use frozen green beans to eliminate the time spent trimming fresh ones.

3   quarts water
1½ pounds fresh green beans
1   large carrot, scraped
¼   cup butter or margarine
½   teaspoon garlic powder
¼   teaspoon dried basil
¼   teaspoon hot sauce
2   tablespoons diced pimiento (optional)
2   teaspoons finely grated lemon rind

Make-Ahead: Bring 3 quarts water to a boil in a Dutch oven. Meanwhile, wash beans; trim ends, and remove strings. Set beans aside.

Cut off and discard ½" from each end of carrot. Using a vegetable peeler, cut 8 paper-thin lengthwise strips from carrot; trim ends evenly. Add carrot strips to boiling water in Dutch oven; cook 45 seconds or just until tender. Remove with a slotted spoon; set aside, and cool.

Return water to a boil, and add beans. Cook 5 minutes or until crisp-tender. Drain; rinse with cold water, and drain. Gather 8 to 12 cooked beans into a bundle; wrap 1 carrot strip around each bundle. Tie ends in a knot, or tuck ends under each bundle and place in a large baking dish.

Melt butter in a small skillet over medium heat. Stir in garlic powder, basil, and hot sauce; cook 30 seconds. Drizzle melted butter mixture over beans. Cover with aluminum foil, and chill up to 1 day.

When Ready to Serve: Bake beans, covered, at 350° for 10 minutes or until thoroughly heated. Sprinkle with pimiento, if desired, and lemon rind before serving. Serve carefully, keeping bundles wrapped with carrot strips.
Yield: 8 servings.

BUNDLING GREEN BEANS

Place about eight green beans on each blanched carrot strip and tie once. Carefully transfer to a baking dish.

STAINED GLASS SALAD

This sparkling gelatin salad will add color to your menu.

1½ cups water
2   (3-ounce) packages sparkling white grape-flavored or lemon-flavored gelatin
2   cups ginger ale, chilled
1   cup red seedless grapes
1   (11-ounce) can mandarin oranges, drained
1   (8¼-ounce) can pineapple tidbits, drained
Green leaf lettuce leaves
Garnish: red seedless grape clusters

Bring water to a boil in a small saucepan; add gelatin, and cook, stirring constantly, 2 minutes or until gelatin dissolves. Chill 15 minutes. Gently stir in cold ginger ale. Cover and chill 1 hour or until consistency of unbeaten egg white. Gently stir 15 seconds. Stir in 1 cup grapes, oranges, and pineapple.

Pour into a lightly oiled 6-cup mold. Cover and chill until firm or up to 3 days ahead. Unmold salad onto a lettuce-lined serving plate. Garnish, if desired. Serve immediately. **Yield:** 8 servings.

PUMPKIN CHESS PIE

For ease, we offer this simple but delicious alternative to Bûche de Noël, the most time-consuming recipe of the menu. If you'd rather spend your time wrapping those last-minute gifts, though, buy a commercial pumpkin pie.

½   (15-ounce) package refrigerated piecrusts
1   (15-ounce) can pumpkin
½   cup half-and-half
3   eggs
1½ teaspoons vanilla extract
2   cups sugar
½   cup plus 1 tablespoon butter or margarine
¾   teaspoon salt
½   teaspoon ground cinnamon
¼   teaspoon ground ginger
¼   teaspoon ground cloves
Praline Sauce

Place piecrust in a 9" pieplate; fold edges under, and crimp. Process pumpkin and next 9 ingredients in container of an electric blender or food processor until smooth, stopping once to scrape down sides.

Pour pumpkin mixture into prepared piecrust. Bake at 350° for 1 hour and 10 minutes or until knife inserted in center comes out clean. Cool completely on a wire rack. Serve with Praline Sauce. **Yield:** 1 (9") pie.

PRALINE SAUCE

This rich sauce is also good spooned over ice cream and is perfect for gift-giving.

1   cup firmly packed brown sugar
½   cup half-and-half
½   cup butter or margarine
½   cup chopped pecans, toasted
½   teaspoon vanilla extract

Combine first 3 ingredients in a small saucepan over medium heat. Bring to a boil; cook, stirring constantly, 1 minute. Remove from heat; stir in pecans and vanilla. Cool slightly; serve warm over slices of pie. **Yield:** 2 cups.

Stained Glass Salad

DECORATING FOR THE HOLIDAYS

Simple materials yield stunning results whether on the front door, the mantel, or the chandelier. Turn the page for some fresh ideas.

DRESSED IN SEASONAL STYLE

"Updating your holiday style doesn't mean throwing out old favorites and buying everything brand-new," says Ray Jordan, a seasoned Christmas decorator and owner of a Christmas specialty shop. "The trick is to find new ways to work with what you already have."

Ray's personal holiday decorating philosophy? "If it's worth doing, it's worth overdoing." And it all starts with the tree.

TREE-TRIMMING TIPS

• Transform your tree into a spectacular Christmas centerpiece by piling on lots of lights and shiny bead garlands.

"Bead garlands give the tree a little sparkle and create a nice scalloped effect," Ray says. "Even if you don't have ornaments, if you put a bead garland and lights on your tree, it looks great."

• Weave strands of lights in and out of the tree as well as around it, stringing them in toward the trunk and out to the branch tips to create depth.

• Use the same strategy when hanging ornaments. Put plain glass balls on branches close to the trunk, and showcase your favorite ornaments near the tips.

• Ray suggests that you secure valuable ornaments to the tree by wiring the hook to the tree branch or tying it on with a sheer red ribbon.

• If you don't want to use a lot of ornaments, you can create an equally festive look by winding lengths of sheer fabric around the tree and in and out of the branches (just like the lights). Try abaca, an open-weave burlap-style fabric, or take apart a grapevine wreath and wind it through the tree for a rustic look.

• Ray prefers an artificial tree so that he can decorate early and because it will hold more and heavier ornaments. "Even if you use an artificial tree," Ray says, "you should have something fresh elsewhere in the house."

Ray Jordan, who never loses the spirit of his favorite season, has an important bit of advice: Cherish the ritual of decorating the tree, of rediscovering favorite ornaments and the memories they evoke. When you've finished decorating, turn off the lights, plug in the tree, and enjoy the season.

STARTING FRESH

Garlands and wreaths—in pine, fir, eucalyptus, cedar, or holly—are an easy way to introduce fresh greenery and fragrance and to accent focal points such as staircases, mantels, mirrors, bookcases, windows, and sideboards. Use decorative ribbon or shimmery fabric to enhance the greenery. Wired ribbon is especially easy to work with and can be used year after year.

For a showy presentation, swag garlands and nestle clusters of berries, ribbons and bows, and strings of lights into the branches. "Little white lights on garlands add a lot of spark to the decorations."

Handmade Christmas tree topiaries studded with vintage beads, buttons, and costume jewelry create an eye-catching arrangement on a mirrored sideboard.

Ray Jordan's pièce de résistance is an abundantly decorated tree adorned with twenty strands of bead garlands, forty strings of lights, and some two thousand ornaments, including an extensive collection of Christopher Radko glass ornaments and souvenirs from Ray's travels.

A profusion of long-stemmed glorioso lilies makes an exceptional centerpiece for the holiday table.
"When I do flowers I do single stems—just lilies or tulips in a vase," Ray says. "A bunch of red tulips
in a vase is just great, and it's elegant and easy to do."

Ray fashions a natural setting for his nativity scene by placing it on a piece of burlap covered with sheet moss (available at craft stores and floral shops) and adding greenery and potted paperwhites.

THE TREE IS ONLY THE BEGINNING

When planning your Christmas decorations, don't forget the rest of the house. "I tell people to look at magazines, see what you like, and then do it," Ray says. "Maybe not with such expensive materials, but with what you already have."

In addition to the festive touches pictured here, Ray offers these suggestions for introducing the spirit of the season: wire fresh fruit to a wreath for a window or door, hang a bay leaf wreath in the kitchen, or string a garland above the stovetop. He also loves filling the house with blooming plants such as paperwhites, hyacinths, amaryllis, and orchids during the holidays.

"A big basket of blooming plants is a great look and will last through the entire season," he says.

Ray recommends using plenty of trimmings to achieve the lavish look that distinguishes a well-dressed holiday home from a house that's simply decorated. "Don't do just a bow on a railing or a door—put some greenery behind it. The difference is amazing."

In Ray Jordan's living room, a tailored stocking on a swagged garland of fresh greenery brightens a bookcase. Lights and ribbon woven through the garland add sparkle.

A Cheery Welcome

A basket of greenery is a fresh change
from the traditional wreath.

Tuck a heavy-duty plastic bag (such as a
zip-top bag) in a basket with a flat back.
Moisten a block of floral foam and place it
inside the plastic bag. Stick greenery clippings into the floral foam. Here we used fir
clippings (from the Christmas tree), varie-
gated holly, berries, and evergreen leaves.
Wire a bow to the basket or to a floral pick
that can be secured in the basket. To make
the bow, see page 153.

GREENERY BY THE YARD

Your own backyard has almost everything you need to create fresh and fragrant trimmings. Our greenery guide on page 33 helps you identify the top Southern plants for holiday decorating.

Fresh materials—magnolia leaves, pine boughs, nandina berries, apples, and oranges—evoke a festive air when snuggled around the candles and punch bowl on an antique jelly cupboard.

Layering simple materials adds up to a grand display. This mantel decoration uses cedar and pine greenery adorned with pinecones, dried hydrangea blooms, and berries. Red pillar candles provide rich color and height.

CANDLELIGHT & MAGNOLIAS

Magnolia leaves are easy to find in the South, and they're easy to arrange, making them a logical material for fresh holiday decorations. With this mantel arrangement, one side of the mantel is the mirror image of the other.

To get this look, partially fill two containers or glass vases with round ornaments. Tuck the stems of magnolia leaves among the ornaments. Add dried seed pods or blooms for texture, if desired. The ornaments will hold the materials in place.

Cluster several pillar candles in the center of the mantel, and fill in with greenery clippings, a bead garland, and ornaments. Place tapers in glass candleholders on each end of the mantel to enhance the balanced effect.

AN ELEGANT GATHERING

This formal arrangement is actually easy to assemble. Start with a decorative (waterproof) container; the urn used here adds height, allowing the lower branches of greenery to fall gracefully over the edge.

Secure a block of moistened floral foam in the bottom of the container. Stick branches of greenery into the floral foam, creating the basic outline of the arrangement. (The one pictured has the shape of a slightly off-center triangle.) Fill in with branches of pine, cedar, magnolia, and holly. Place clusters of nandina berries among the greenery branches to add a spark of contrasting color.

31

GILT TOPIARIES

Moss topiaries are easy to make and to individualize with leaves and berries that have been spray-painted gold. Push a sturdy, straight twig found in your backyard into the bottom of a Styrofoam ball to form a topiary. Secure the topiary in a terra-cotta pot that is filled with a Styrofoam or floral foam block. (For more stability, hot-glue the block to the bottom of the pot.) Using thick white craft glue, cover the ball and the top of the base with sheet moss.

Gather leaves, berries, and twigs from your yard. Spray them with gold paint, and hot-glue them to the topiary. Finish by gluing on bows or lengths of ribbon.

EVERGREEN GARLAND

A garland wrapped with wired ribbon gracefully festoons the mantelpiece and fills the room with the unmistakable scent of cedar. Here a deep firebox keeps flames well away from the greenery, something to keep in mind when placing decorations near a fireplace or candles.

Use floral wire to attach the bow to the garland. To make the garland and bow, see pages 146 and 153.

WINTER GREENERY CUTTING GUIDE

You'll be surprised at the amount of decorating material you can gather from your own backyard. Here are some native Southern plants whose clippings work beautifully in holiday arrangements. Before cutting, consider how the plant will grow after pruning and make your cuts to maintain the natural form of the plant.

NANDINA
Grape-like clusters of red berries make nandina one of the most sought after plants for seasonal clippings. The berries add bright color and texture to wreaths, centerpieces, and mantel decorations.

MAGNOLIA
Glossy green magnolia leaves are a traditional holiday favorite. Use clusters of leaves on mantels or sideboards, or pin them individually to a wreath form.

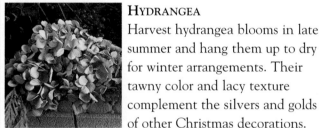

HYDRANGEA
Harvest hydrangea blooms in late summer and hang them up to dry for winter arrangements. Their tawny color and lacy texture complement the silvers and golds of other Christmas decorations.

AUCUBA
The yellowish green leaves of aucuba offer an attractive contrast to the darker green leaves of magnolia and holly.

HOLLY
Dark green leaves and brilliant red berries make this the quintessential holiday greenery. Use clippings of holly to add seasonal sparkle to any arrangement.

A HARVEST FOR THE EYES AND SPIRIT

Welcome to the Grove Park Inn, where the Bountiful Harvest Tree, inspired by the region's apple harvest and farmers markets, offers ideas aplenty.

Whether you need a simple tree or dramatic focal point, the Bountiful Harvest Tree shown at left will inspire you. Its designer, David Santana, could pass for a cast member of the Broadway musical *Grease*. Although he is actually the visual arts and floral manager for the Grove Park Inn, David does have a gift for the dramatic.

David and his staff decorate forty uniquely designed trees throughout the inn for Christmas and style settings for parties and celebrations throughout the New Year, too. (He's been working on ideas for the millennium New Year's event since last Christmas.) But he still has time to share his ideas and a few hints on the next pages.

Baskets spilling with fruit add motion and whimsy to the tree's decorations.

The Grove Park Inn, built at the turn of the century, overlooks Asheville, North Carolina, and the Blue Ridge mountains. As one travel writer says, "It's a wonderful place to call home for the holidays."

David Santana invites you to a fireside chat. The topic? His Bountiful Harvest Tree created especially for our readers.

Tied to the tree with raffia, a basket filled with shiny apples brightens a dark spot.

STEP-BY-STEP TO A BEAUTIFUL, BOUNTIFUL TREE

These tips are from a tree decorating pro. David's secret: "Use more than you think you will need. Abundance is the key."

- First place **white icicle lights** in the tree's interior to lend a shimmery foil for the **yellow lights** that spiral along the tree's outer branches.

- For a garland, wind split strands of yellow-gold **burlap** into the tree, starting at the top and placing it deep into the branches.

- For the tree topper, insert 2'-long sticks of **curly willow** spray-painted gold and copper.

- Tie **baskets** filled with excelsior to the tree with raffia. (Floral wire helps secure the baskets, if needed.) Use light-colored excelsior for dark baskets, darker excelsior for light baskets. Tie 5 or 6 strands of **raffia** around the basket handles, allowing ribbons of raffia to cascade from the handle.

"Cheat your eye and tilt the baskets out. Place them at whimsical angles. You want lots of movement." Then fill the baskets with **plastic fruit,** securing the fruit with floral wire. Place light fruit in any dark spots to catch the light. You can use any fruit—strawberries, pomegranates, apples, grapes, etc.

- Next, add the **ornaments** and bunch **fabric** at the base of the tree to make the skirt.

- Additional strands of **icicle lights** in the lowest branches of the tree add light at the tree's base and intermingle with gifts.

PUT-A-LID-ON-IT ORNAMENT

Make a tassel as described in Step 1 for the Blackberry Ornament (facing page). Glue the tassel to the bottom of a canning jar lid. Make a loop and glue it to the top of the lid; this makes the hanger. Write a holiday greeting with a permanent marker on the front of the lid (see ornaments, right). These fun baubles also make great package labels.

THE BLACKBERRY ORNAMENT

David Santana's Blackberry Ornament adds personality to the Bountiful Harvest Tree. A family keepsake ornament inspired him to use canning jar rings as the main material.

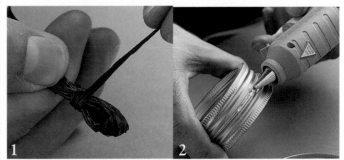

1. Make a tassel by cutting 3 or more lengths of raffia and doubling them over. Wrap and tie a piece of raffia around the top to create the "head" of the tassel. Clip any leftover wrapped raffia and dab the tie with hot glue to secure.

2. Glue 2 canning jar rings together to make the frame of the ornament.

3. Tie 2 (12"-15") pieces of raffia together at each end (this makes the raffia easy to hold). Wrap the raffia around the outside edge of the canning jar rings, securing with glue in at least 4 spots. Thread a piece of raffia through what you've just secured and tie it off to make a hanger for the ornament.

4. Place a sprig of blackberries (or any ornamentation of your choice) to the side of the ring. Hot-glue the fruit to the rings. Cover spots of glue with leaves.

5. Place a dot of glue inside the top of the rings. Press the tassel into the glue to secure. Let dry.

FOCUS ON THE FIREPLACE

Whether you prefer lush greens and holiday reds or dramatic metallics and crisp whites, these five mantel decorating ideas here and on the following pages will inspire you to make the most of this cozy focal point.

Tuck two ornamental cabbages (with stems trimmed) into the garland at the center of the mantel. Fill in along the rest of the mantel with berries you gather from your yard, such as holly or nandina berries.

Roses are expensive, but if you're hosting several gatherings, they're worth the price—and they will stay beautiful and fresh for several days.

LUSH AND LOVELY

An evergreen garland that trails along the mantel and down the sides to rest on the floor is the starting point for this dramatic setting. The elaborate look, however, belies its simplicity. It takes just a few carefully chosen pieces to create this beautiful decoration.

Vases of red roses anchor the arrangement and can last up to a week. If you prefer, use poinsettias in place of the roses for a less expensive and longer-lasting option. Burgundy-tinged leaves enhance and lend depth to the rich, red color scheme.

Rosebud wreaths accent the garland at each end of the mantel. To make each wreath, stick rosebuds and sprigs of greenery, berries, and seeded eucalyptus into a moistened oasis wreath form. Or use evergreen wreaths adorned with wired-on red berries as an alternative. For the stockings and materials, see Sources, page 154.

A moistened base keeps the wreath fresh at least a week.

PRETTY AND PLAYFUL

This festive assemblage includes a teapot and teacup, pepper berries, poinsettias, and candles. Ornaments nestled among the berries reflect the candlelight's warm glow.

At each end of the mantel, 12" wreaths are hung with a thin wire and attached with double-sided mounting tape. A star-shaped wreath covered with pepper berries is in the center. To make the wreaths shown here, either hot-glue or wire pepper berries, cranberry-colored dried flowers, dried rosebuds, and dried pomegranates to a floral foam wreath form. For some of the materials shown here, see Sources, page 154.

Candy canes fill cranberry-colored drinking glasses, while glass votive holders and candles add a welcome sparkle.

The kitchen cupboard offers delightfully unexpected decorating objects, such as this teapot and cup.

ARTFUL AND ABUNDANT

Clippings from your backyard and fruit from the local grocery are the main ingredients for this variation on a Della Robbia theme. Large clusters of broad magnolia leaves and lacy cedar branches, layered so that all of the stems are covered, form the backdrop for grapes, pears, and green apples.

A wicker basket tree is filled with fruit, providing an eye-catching anchor for the mantel arrangement. Other types of tall containers such as a clear vase or a metal urn will serve the same function.

Bold green-and-cream candles are placed in metal urns and surrounded by plump red grapes. For the candles, see Sources, page 154.

Green apples are cleverly hollowed out to make room for small tea light candles. Glittering gold ribbon winds gracefully around the fruit and along the length of the mantel.

SUBTLE AND SOPHISTICATED

Key elements in soft tones of gold and silver convey a glamorous holiday ambience. The mantel scarf is made by layering shimmery raw silk dinner napkins, points down, on top of the mantel. Clear and beaded votive holders and silver julep cups and glasses filled with candy canes hold the napkins in place. A gold bead garland and gold ornaments unify all the pieces. For the initial ornaments and other items used here, see Sources, page 154.

Initial ornaments, hanging from ribbons looped over the votive holders, add a personal touch.

Gaily wrapped boxes are easy to do and inexpensive, and they make a big impact in your decorations, as on this mantel where they are a focal point.

42

WHITE AND BRIGHT

Dreams of a white Christmas come true with the frosty combination of white and silver. On this mantel, white pillar candles and white, clear, and silver containers set the wintry mood. Angel hair creates a soft cloud along the top of the mantel. Large white snowflakes and pearl-white ornaments are suspended by ribbons at varying lengths, giving an interesting finish.

The topiary is made by hot-gluing small pearl-white orna-ments on a Styrofoam tree form. Set the tree on a small compote or dish, or place it directly on top of the mantel.

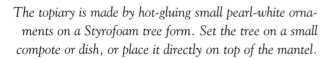

OVER-the-TOP HOLIDAY STYLE

Take your holiday decorations to new heights. Here are three variations that will work on most styles of chandeliers.

▲ ANGELIC ADDITIONS

The chandelier treatment shown here is done in the same way as the one pictured opposite and described below, omitting the garland. Two- to 3"-wide wired ribbon drapes gracefully around the lights, with ribbon bows tied at each candle's base. Papier-mâché angel ornaments are tied around the bottom of the light with ribbons.

◀ BOW BEAUTIFUL

This greenery-and-ribbon bedecked chandelier starts with a fresh mixed garland draped around the chandelier and secured with floral wire. Ribbon and bows are fancy embellishments to the plain garland. (Wired ribbon gives the best result because it holds its shape.) Weave the ribbon around the garland and add fluffy bows at the base of each light. Tie the bows on with ribbon or a short piece of floral wire. The ribbon pictured is 3" wide.

For the chandelier top, make 2 or 3 bows and wire them and lengths of ribbon streamers to trail down the light's chain. To make a bow, see page 153.

▲ SIMPLY ORNAMENTAL

Here's a perfect way to display your favorite vintage ornaments. Loop lengths of ¾"-wide ribbon through the ornaments and tie them to the base of the chandelier at varying lengths. Tie 3"-wide wired ribbon streamers to the chandelier's chain. Use narrow ribbon or floral wire to affix ornaments along the chain.

Hang votive holders made from baby food jars among the ornaments. Place a tea light (with the metal base removed) in each jar. To make the votive holders, see page 146.

CHRISTMAS BY CANDLELIGHT

*Candles lend extra sparkle to holiday decorations and create a
warm and festive mood. Gather plain white pillars and colorful tapers;
the photos on these pages will fill you with bright ideas on how to use them.*

PINECONE CANDLE RINGS ▲

Pinecone wreaths lend an outdoorsy look to white candles.
To form the pinecone candle rings, find a jar lid that is an
appropriate size to act as a holder for a pillar candle. Trace
around the lid on a piece of cardboard. (A discarded cardboard box is ideal.) Draw another circle 1" larger around the
traced circle. Cut out the cardboard around the outside circle. Glue the jar lid with lip facing up in the center of the
cardboard circle. Spray-paint the lid and circle gold.
Arrange pinecones in a ring around the jar lid/candleholder.
Hot-glue the pinecones to the cardboard. Let dry. Lightly
apply gold paint, such as Treasure Gold or Rub 'n Buff, to
the tips of the pinecones, if desired. Let dry.

CANDLES IN SNOW ▲

Crystalline rock salt makes an elegant base for silver
tapers. Create a variety of looks with different shapes and
styles of glass vases, dishes, and bowls.

MOSS AND RIBBON CANDLEHOLDERS ▶

Made from permanent materials, these candleholders can be
used year after year. To make a base so that the moss candleholder will fit in a conventional candlestick, push a 2"-3"
nail through the small end of a cork that fits into the
candlestick. Insert the nail with the cork into the bottom
of a Styrofoam ball. Insert a plastic candleholder into the
top of the Styrofoam ball (opposite the cork).

   Cover the Styrofoam ball with sheet moss, using either
glue or floral pins. Glue or pin ribbons and permanent
fruit and foliage to the ball for embellishment.

FLOATING CANDLES

Floating candles are a great idea for a cocktail party or Christmas Eve buffet: float candles in small punch bowls filled with water and a sprinkling of metallic confetti. A garland, ornaments, and votive holders carry out the gold-hued theme.

GILT-LEAF CANDLE POTS ▶

Make unique candleholders by spray-painting leaves in metallic hues and hot-gluing them around terra-cotta pots. Velvety ribbons tied around the pots help hold the leaves in place and add complementary color.

SILVER-TRIMMED PILLARS ▼

Adorn plain pillar candles with silver beads and trims. Group several on a mantel or sideboard surrounded by a pretty garland of ribbon, fabric, or greenery. Beaded chain (found at hardware stores) is secured with a dot of hot glue at the beginning and end of the chain, which is wound around one candle's base. For the other candles, fabric cording and ribbons are easy embellishments that can be secured with hot glue or straight pins.

BEYOND RED AND GREEN

For a jazzy change of pace, let jewel-toned decorations set the holiday table.

*U*pstage the traditional color scheme of Christmas with richly colored garlands and ornaments in vivid jewel tones. The assembly of the fashionable approach shown here is easy—it's all in the details, each reinforcing the unique tones of the overall arrangement.

Trail a simple beaded garland down the center of a luxurious swath of regal purple fabric to become the focal point on the dining table. Tuck under the raw ends of the fabric and fill the tabletop with cranberry, pistachio green, and violet glassware brimming with flowers and ornaments. Add sparkling votives for just the right amount of twinkle.

For extraordinary place cards (above), trim colored paper with decorative-edge scissors and wire the personalized tags to round ornaments. Tie the ornaments to the arms of the chandelier with sheer ribbon. For the garland and ornaments, see Sources, page 154.

DECORATING WITH FRUIT

Rich colors and attractive shapes and textures make seasonal fruits a natural centerpiece of your holiday decor.

A fruited chandelier swag crowns the dining room. To make the swag, thread kumquats, crab apples, kumquat leaves, and dried orange slices on floral wire. Leave a few inches of wire at the end of each strand and use it to attach the swag to the chandelier. Finish the look by weaving strands of ribbon through the arms of the fixture.

DRYING CITRUS FRUIT

Place sliced fruit on a wire rack on top of a cookie sheet and place it in a 200° oven. Leave the fruit in the oven for 6 to 10 hours or until the fruit is leathery. (The drying time will vary with the type of fruit, the thickness of the slices, and the humidity.) Remove the fruit from the oven, and let it air-dry on the rack until it is dry to the touch.

Seasonal fruit adds a festive touch. Tie fresh oranges and limes with wired ribbon. Use upholstery tacks to hold the ribbon in place and to release the citrusy scent. Arrange the fruit in your prettiest china bowl or tureen for a simple centerpiece.

Limes and fresh greenery wired to a grapevine wreath convey a fragrant welcome. Any type of evergreen clippings from your backyard will work here. To secure the limes to the wreath, insert a floral pick into the fruit. Twist the wire at the other end of the pick around the wreath. Find floral picks and vine wreaths at discount, craft, and import stores.

A holiday arrangement need not be elaborate to be beautiful. Here, kumquats and wild yaupon berries are charming companions in a glass vase.

Lemon leaves tucked into a floral foam wreath create a festive frame for a large pillar candle. To protect tabletops and to make the piece easy to move, place the wreath form on a large plate. Circle the candle with small crab apples, cherries, and kumquats.

Place a glass bowl in the center of an evergreen wreath. Put a few green apples in the bowl and fill in around the apples with fresh cranberries. Add the candles. The cranberries and apples will hold the candles in place.

BEADS WORK

A classic holiday embellishment for sweaters and shoes, beads also add sparkle and shine to everything from napkin rings to candles.

NAPKIN RINGS

Place the accent on elegance by tying beaded tassels to ribbon or decorative wire and wrapping around dinner napkins.

To make the tassels, string assorted beads on 15 lengths (approximately 7" each) of fishing line, tying knots in the bottom of the lines to hold the beads and leaving 4" of line free at the top. Using the line at the top of each length, knot the beaded lengths together to form a tassel.

To make the tassel top, knot a length (approximately 5" long) of fishing line around a jump ring (found at craft and discount stores), and string assorted beads on the line, leaving 3" of line free. Tie the free end of line to the tassel, joining the tassel and tassel top together. Trim the excess fishing line from the knot. Thread ribbon or decorative wire through the jump ring, and tie or wrap the beaded napkin ring around a napkin.

ICICLE ORNAMENTS

Colored beads strung on wire make fanciful dangling ornaments to hang on the tree, in a window, or along a ribbon for a miniature garland.

To make an icicle ornament, hold one end of a 12" length of 20-gauge brass wire with needlenose pliers. Wrap the wire around the pliers to form a spiral, leaving 2" of wire free at the end. Gently open the spiral to form a loose cone shape.

On a 6" length of 24-gauge copper wire, thread an assortment of beads (forming a length of beads about 3" long), twisting one end of the wire to hold the beads in place and leaving the other end free.

Insert one end of the spiral-shaped wire into the second bead from the bottom on the beaded wire. Twirl the beaded wire around the spiral wire so the beads are at the center of the spiral. (You may need to adjust the size of the spirals to allow room for the beads to fit.) Twist the two free ends of wire together, curving them to form a hook for hanging.

BEADED CANDLES

Put square candles in a party mood by dressing them with beads. For materials, see Sources, page 154.

For the tall candle, draw two trees with the point of a straight pin or a pencil. With straight pins and a thimble, press pins through small beads into the candle, filling in the tree design. Pin a sequin star at the top.

For the rectangle candle, with straight pins and a thimble, press a pin through a white 4mm bead and a 1" snowflake sequin into the candle. Repeat on all sides of the candle. Pin single beads in between the snowflakes.

For the square candle, glue or pin 10mm emerald rhinestones and 12mm red rhinestones in the pattern of your choice.

NO-SEW NOEL

Here's an easy way to make holiday must-haves without breaking out the needle and thread.

You'll want to make lots of these ornaments to give as gifts and to use as package toppers.
Turn the page for instructions for the ornaments, stocking, and a tree skirt.

NO-SEW NOEL ORNAMENTS

patterns on pages 149-150
2 (9" x 12") rectangles red felt
2 (9" x 12") rectangles black felt
1 small package (three 6½" x 9" sheets) instant stick &
 hold sheet adhesive for fabric (we used Coats)
4 (8mm) red sequins
10 rocaille beads
black dimensional paint pen
6 (10mm) black sequins
black buttonhole thread

1. Following manufacturer's directions, affix sheet adhesive to the black felt and to the red felt.

2. Trace and cut out the patterns for the bird, urns, and wing. Using the patterns and following the directions on the pattern pages, cut 4 birds and 2 urns from the red felt; cut 4 wings and 2 urns from the black felt.

3. For the bird ornament: Peel the backing from the adhesive on the back of a red bird cutout and affix the bird to a larger piece of black felt. (A straight pin helps peel the adhesive backing from the felt.) Cut the black felt, leaving a ¼" border around the bird.

4. Affix a second red bird to the back of the black shape. Peel the backing from the adhesive on a black wing cutout and affix the wing to the bird front. Repeat for the bird back. Following manufacturer's directions, fuse the pieces together.

5. Glue or sew 1 red sequin with a rocaille bead to each side of the bird ornament to make eyes.

6. Using a paint pen, draw 3 lines on the bird tail. Let dry. Repeat on the other side of the bird. Let dry.

7. For the urn ornament: Peel the backing from the adhesive on one of the red urn shapes. Affix it to second red urn shape.

8. Peel the backing from the adhesive on one of the black urn shapes. Affix it to one side of the red urn. Affix the second black urn to the other side.

9. Referring to the photograph, glue or sew 3 black sequins with rocaille beads to each side of the ornament.

10. Using a paint pen, draw flower stems and leaves on the urn. Let dry. Repeat on the other side of urn. Let dry.

11. Thread a 10" length of buttonhole thread through each ornament top to make a hanger. Tie the thread ends.

NO-SEW NOEL STOCKING

patterns and diagram on page 148
red felt (18" x 24")
1 sheet (6½" x 9") instant stick & hold sheet adhesive
 for fabric (we used Coats)
black felt (9" x 12")
11 rocaille beads
9 (10mm) black sequins
hot-glue gun and glue sticks
1 package black extra-wide double fold bias tape (we
 used Wright's)

1. Trace and cut out the stocking pattern. Using the pattern, cut two stockings from red felt.

2. Following manufacturer's directions, affix the sheet adhesive to the black felt.

3. Trace and cut out the patterns for the bird, leaves, and branches. Using the patterns and following the directions on the pattern page, cut out the birds, leaves, and branches from the black felt.

4. Referring to the photograph, position the cutouts on the stocking top. When satisfied with the placement, peel the backing from the sheet adhesive and affix the cutouts to the stocking. (A straight pin helps peel the adhesive backing from the felt.) Following manufacturer's directions, fuse the cutouts to the stocking.

5. Referring to the photograph, glue or sew one rocaille bead to each bird to make an eye. Arrange three sequins at the end of each branch. Glue or sew the sequins to the stocking with one rocaille bead for each sequin.

6. Using a hot-glue gun, attach the stocking front to the stocking back, gluing around the outside edges only and leaving the top open.

7. Open the bias tape. Beginning at the top left of the stocking, glue one side of the bias tape to the front of the stocking, leaving ½" of the tape extending from the left top of the stocking and 16" extending from the right top of the stocking (see diagram, page 148). Turn the stocking over; glue the tape to the stocking back.

8. On the left side of the stocking, fold the ½" overlap of bias tape to the inside of the stocking and glue in place. On the right side of the stocking, fold the 16" length of bias tape in half and glue the raw edge inside the stocking to make a hanger.

NO-SEW NOEL TREE SKIRT

patterns and diagram on pages 150-151

red felt (50" x 50")

hot-glue gun and glue sticks

4 yards black double fold bias quilt binding (we used
   Wright's)

1 yard black extra-wide double fold bias tape (we used
   Wright's)

1 yard (36" wide) black felt

2 large packages (13½" x 30" sheet in each) instant
   stick & hold sheet adhesive for fabric (we used
   Coats)

16 rocaille beads

12 (10mm) black sequins

1. To cut a 45" diameter circle, fold the felt square into
quarters. Using a yardstick, pivot the measuring stick from
the center fold, chalking a line that is half the diameter of
the desired circle. Cut along the chalked line through all 4
layers of felt. Cut a 10" diameter circle from the center of
the skirt, following previous instructions. Use a yardstick

and chalk to draw a straight line from the outer edge to
the inner circle. Cut along the straight chalk line.

2. Using a glue gun, attach the quilt binding to the
perimeter of the tree skirt and attach the bias tape to
the perimeter of the inner circle opening.

3. Following manufacturer's directions, affix sheet adhesive to several large pieces of black felt and to a 6" x 8"
piece of red felt. Trace and cut out all tree skirt patterns.
Using patterns, cut out the designs.

4. To position the designs on the tree skirt, picture the
tree skirt as a clock. Referring to the diagram on page
151, place one urn each at 3:00, 6:00, and 9:00. Place the
4 birds and branches at Xs as indicated on the diagram.

5. When the designs are in the desired positions, peel the
backing from the adhesive on the backs of the designs. (A
straight pin helps peel the adhesive backing from the
felt.) Following manufacturer's directions, affix designs to
one section of the tree skirt at a time.

6. Glue or sew one rocaille bead to each bird to make an
eye. Arrange three sequins at the end of each branch.
Glue or sew sequins with rocaille beads to the tree skirt.

PEPPERMINT TWIST

You can do a lot more with candy canes than simply eat them. Enjoy new ways to make these classic Christmas treats a part of your decorating scheme. Kids (and kids at heart) will love them.

◀ CANDY CANE TOWER

This centerpiece will be a sweet reminder of the holidays all season long. To assemble the tower, get three plastic ice cream containers—large, medium, and small. (Empty containers can be bought for under $1.00 at most ice cream shops.) Referring to the photograph, glue an assortment of candy canes around the large and medium containers. Glue peppermint sticks around the small container. Stack the containers from large to small, gluing the container tops to the container bottoms to hold the tower in place. Fill in along the outside rims between the containers with small peppermint candies. Stack more peppermints on the top of the tower to cover the container's lid. Tie a ribbon around the centerpiece, if desired.

This container is a real treat. Glue candy canes around a clean, unused paint bucket. (Unused paint buckets can be purchased from most paint stores for around $1.00.) Fill the bucket with peppermint candies, and you have a candy dish that doubles as a bright holiday decoration. For a quick and inexpensive gift, wrap clear cellophane around the candy-filled bucket and tie it at the top with red ribbon.

PEPPERMINT TREE

Family and friends can pluck candy straight from this tree. Royal Icing holds the peppermints on the topiary form so they remain edible.

To make the tree, place a Styrofoam tree with base form in a container. Prepare Royal Icing using the recipe given below. Starting at the bottom of the tree and working in sections, cover the form with Royal Icing and press candies into the icing to secure them. Continue until you have covered the entire tree with icing and candies. Cover the surface of the tree base with Royal Icing and press candies on top, if desired. If the candy canes are heavy, be sure to secure the tips of their hooks with icing at the bottom of the tree for more stability.

For the tree shown, we first trimmed the sticks of lollipops, pushed one into the tip of the tree to form a tree topper, and pushed the other sticks into the Styrofoam base around the trunk of the tree. For the topiary form, see Sources, page 154.

ROYAL ICING

Royal Icing dries to a smooth, hard finish. This edible icing dries very quickly, so keep it covered with a damp cloth at all times.

3   tablespoons commercial meringue powder (available at stores that carry cake decorating supplies)
¼   cup plus 2 tablespoons warm water
1   (16-ounce) package powdered sugar, sifted

Combine meringue powder and water in a large mixing bowl. Beat at medium speed of an electric mixer until frothy. Add half of powdered sugar, mixing well. Add remaining sugar, and beat at high speed 5 to 7 minutes. **Yield:** about 2 cups.

PEPPERMINT PARTY FAVORS

This bubbly presentation of take-home treats for holiday visitors is a cinch to make. Cover a block of Styrofoam with bubble wrap, gathering the bubble wrap at the top of the block and tying it with ribbon. Use straight pins to help hold the wrapping in place; be sure to leave an opening in the gathers at the top of the block for the candy. Push candy canes and peppermint lollipops into the opening at the top of the Styrofoam block, arranging the candy as desired.

65

ALL DRESSED UP

Transform ordinary stockings by adding fancy trims or replacing the cuff with fabric for a totally new look.

FRINGED CUFF

Purchase an inexpensive stocking. If the stocking has a cuff, cut it off at the top of the stocking. Cut 3 yards of 1½"-wide wired black check ribbon into 10" lengths. Fold each length in half, forming a loop. Place the ribbon loops side by side, aligning the raw edges with the top of the stocking. Glue the ribbons in place. Using a doubled length of black thread, tie 1 small jingle bell to the black check ribbon at the center fold.

Cut 1¼ yards of 1½"-wide wired red ribbon into 3½" lengths. Place 1 raw edge of each ribbon length along the top of the stocking, aligning the ribbon lengths side by side. Glue the ribbons in place. Apply liquid ravel preventer to the loose end of each ribbon length. Let dry.

Cut 2 yards of 1"-wide embroidered ribbon into 3" lengths, trimming one end to a point. Apply liquid ravel preventer to the pointed end. Let dry. Place the ribbon lengths side by side, aligning the straight edges with the top of the stocking. Add or overlap pieces to create the desired fullness in the fringe. Glue in place.

Glue an 18" length of gold trim along the top edge of the stocking, covering the raw edges of the ribbons.

TASSELS AND HOLLY CUFF

Purchase an inexpensive stocking. Make a hanging loop by doubling an 18" length of cording with tassel ends. Knot the cord. Glue the knot to the outside of the cuff at the seam.

Use wire cutters to cut gold berries from floral picks. Glue the berries onto the stocking cuff as desired. Cut silk holly leaves and berries from floral picks. Arrange the leaves and berries around the knot in the cord. Glue them in place.

Fringed Cuff

BUTTON CUFF

Purchase an inexpensive stocking. If the stocking has a cuff, cut it off at the top of the stocking. From a fabric remnant, cut a 7"-wide piece that will fit around the top edge of the stocking and overlap slightly. Also from the fabric remnant, cut a 2" x 10" strip for the hanging loop.

With the wrong sides together, fold the fabric for the cuff in half lengthwise, creasing it at the fold. Tuck the top half of the folded fabric piece into the top of the stocking, aligning the center fold along the top of the

Tassels and
Holly Cuff

Button Cuff

stocking and overlapping the fabric edges. Glue the fabric
on the inside of the stocking. Turn the fabric on the outside of the stocking under at the bottom edge and glue to
the stocking, forming a finished edge.

For the hanging loop, fold the long edges of the fabric
strip toward the center. Glue the edges in place. Fold the
fabric strip in half with the glued edges on the inside of the
loop. Tuck the raw ends of the loop inside the stocking
cuff. Glue it in place. Sew buttons along the bottom of the
cuff as desired.

HOLIDAY FARE

*Delectable food is a hallmark of the holiday season.
From appetizers to desserts, the following recipes
will prepare you for every course.*

MEMORIES FROM CHRISTMAS KITCHENS

So many wonderful Christmas memories are cooked up in the kitchen. But when you work around food almost 365 days a year, as these food journalists do, the rituals of preparing holiday fare—and the people doing the cooking— become more precious than the finished treats.

Skillet Full of Love

I remember my grandmother lifting the lid off a deep cast-iron skillet of sautéed quail she'd prepared for Christmas dinner. I'd never had quail before, and the rich, woodsy aroma was unbelievable. I helped her make the gravy to go with it. I never eat quail without thinking about her love for cooking.

Denise Gee
Associate Foods Editor, *Southern Living* magazine

NANNIE'S SMOTHERED QUAIL

6	dressed quail
⅔	cup all-purpose flour
¾	teaspoon salt
¾	teaspoon ground black pepper
½	teaspoon Cajun seasoning
⅛	teaspoon ground red pepper
¾	cup vegetable oil
2	cups water

Split quail lengthwise to, but not through, breast bone; spread quail open, and pat dry. Combine flour and next 4 ingredients; dredge quail in flour mixture, reserving flour mixture.

Pour oil into a 12" cast-iron skillet. Fry quail in 2 batches in hot oil over medium heat 3 to 4 minutes or until browned. Remove quail, and set aside. Reserve ¼ cup drippings in skillet.

Add reserved flour mixture to drippings. Cook, stirring constantly, 4 minutes or until flour is browned. Slowly add water, stirring constantly. Return quail to skillet; bring to a boil. Cover, reduce heat, and simmer 20 minutes or until quail is tender and gravy is thickened. Serve quail with gravy over wild rice blend, dirty rice, or mashed potatoes. **Yield:** 2 to 3 servings.

The rich, woodsy aroma of Nannie's Smothered Quail brings back fond memories of Grandmother to Denise Gee.

Forever and a Duck

One of my most memorable Christmas dinners centered on a trio of Ducklings a l'Orange that ended up taking us most of the day to prepare. The long list of ingredients and a multistep preparation procedure have become more memorable than the end product. We enjoyed the shared effort as the

recipe's complicated steps slowly became humorous (as in "oh no, you mean we first have to make a stock?") Now that I think of it, I believe it was a recipe from Julia Child.

Kate Greer
Editor, *Weight Watchers* magazine

Sentimental Sandwich

My mother always baked a ham on Christmas Eve afternoon to take to my grandparent's house on Christmas Day. Though it was to serve along with the chicken and dressing, she always sliced just enough of the warm ham to make sandwiches for dinner. The scent of a ham baking and a warm ham sandwich always mean Christmas Eve to me.

Diane Hogan
Assistant Foods Editor, *Southern Living* magazine

So Many Sisters . . .

For Christmas, I always got a box of homemade chocolate chip cookies from my Aunt Gladys. They were like gold, and after sharing a few—with five sisters, that's one cookie each—I would rush to my room to hide the rest. My aunt is older now and no longer cooks, but she shared her secret recipe

with my wife. The cookies aren't quite the same, but they are almost as good—and still no sharing, please!

Joe Watts
Assistant Editor, *Weight Watchers* magazine

AUNT GLADYS' CHOCOLATE CHIP COOKIES

½   cup butter, softened
¼   cup plus 2 tablespoons sugar
¼   cup plus 2 tablespoons firmly packed brown sugar
½   teaspoon vanilla extract
1   large egg
1   cup plus 2 tablespoons all-purpose flour
½   teaspoon baking soda
½   teaspoon salt
½   cup chopped pecans
1   (6-ounce) package semisweet chocolate morsels

Beat butter and sugars at medium speed of an electric mixer until creamy; add vanilla and egg, beating until blended.

Combine flour, soda, and salt; add to butter mixture, mixing well. Stir in pecans and chocolate morsels. Drop dough by heaping teaspoonfuls onto greased cookie sheets. Bake at 350° for 8 to 10 minutes. Cool slightly on cookie sheets; transfer cookies to wire racks to cool completely. **Yield:** 5 dozen.

Same Time Next Year

Our family always holds its family reunion the Saturday before Christmas. Because the date never changes, invitations really aren't necessary, which makes holiday planning easier for the family.

We decided years ago to forgo the exchanging of gifts, so the reunion centers around the meal. And the menu stays the same year after year. Nothing really fancy, just good food. Most of the dishes bring back memories of growing up, especially for my aunts and uncles—white beans, cornbread, and mashed potatoes.

I've now taken over my mother's responsibilities of roasting the turkey and making the dressing and gravy. My sisters chop the onions and celery while I make the cornbread. Once I have everything mixed together, it's sampling time. Whoever is around at this critical moment gets to taste the dressing and comment on its seasoning—more poultry seasoning, what about a little black pepper, it's too dry, add more turkey broth. Once everyone is satisfied with the flavor, I continue with the recipe. I shape the dressing into pones and bake them on baking sheets. No matter how much I make, it's never enough! If I had a nickel for every pone of dressing I've shaped over the years, I could retire!

My immediate family has always eaten a hearty breakfast on Christmas morning before opening our gifts. Part of my father's Christmas present from me is to prepare this meal. The star of the meal is fried pig's feet. It's a two-day process to cook the feet, and it's worth every minute. I've perfected the preparation and cooking techniques over the years. Friends and neighbors drop by for a sample. Because it's a once-a-year food, it's become a big deal; we talk about it throughout the year, which helps whet our appetites for it.

Kathy Eakin
Senior Foods Editor, Oxmoor House

Custard Is for Children

Boiled custard means Christmas in my family. First it's served formally at the dinner table, but later, leftovers are put on the bottom shelf of the refrigerator in a large bowl with a teacup so that the children can help themselves.

Virginia Cravens
Photo Stylist, Oxmoor House

BOILED CUSTARD

4	cups milk
6	large egg yolks
¾	cup sugar
2	tablespoons cornstarch

Dash of salt

2	teaspoons vanilla extract

Ground nutmeg

Pour milk into top of a double boiler; bring water to a boil. Heat milk until tiny bubbles begin to appear around edges of pan. Remove from heat, and set aside.

Beat egg yolks with a wire whisk until frothy. Add sugar, cornstarch, and salt, beating until thickened. Gradually stir about 1 cup hot milk into yolk mixture; add to remaining milk, stirring constantly.

Cook custard mixture in double boiler over low heat 25 minutes or until mixture is thickened and a candy thermometer registers 180°, stirring occasionally. (Do not boil.) Stir in vanilla. Serve warm or cold; sprinkle with nutmeg. **Yield:** 4 cups.

It Is More Blessed to Give . . .

As a child, I watched my mom prepare dozens of different kinds of candies and cookies to give away in decorative baskets and trays as Christmas gifts. (Of course, we ate our share of the goodies, too!) Our kitchen was too small to hold all the trays of sweets as they were finished, so I remember the wonderful scents of chocolate that filled the air when we would open the door to the back bedroom where Mom would hide them—with only a wood-burning stove to heat the house, that bedroom was like a walk-in refrigerator when the door was shut!

Kathleen Phillips
Test Kitchens Director, Oxmoor House

Kathleen Phillips packs her mom's recipe for Peanut Butter Crunch Candy to give at Christmas. She suggests that if you don't want to take the time to completely coat the candy with chocolate, sprinkle 1½ cups semisweet chocolate morsels over candy immediately after scoring. The hot candy will melt the morsels; then spread it with a knife. Cut through chocolate and candy when cooled.

PEANUT BUTTER CRUNCH CANDY

This candy will remind you of a famous candy bar.

1   cup creamy peanut butter
1   cup sugar
⅓   cup water
⅓   cup light corn syrup
1   (12-ounce) package semisweet chocolate morsels, melted

Butter an 8" square pan.

   Heat peanut butter in top of a double boiler or on low heat in a medium saucepan, stirring constantly, until softened; set aside.

   Combine sugar, water, and syrup in a small saucepan. Cook over medium heat, stirring constantly, until sugar is dissolved. Cover and cook 2 to 3 minutes to wash crystals from sides of pan. Uncover and cook, without stirring, to 310° (hard-crack stage), about 16 minutes.

   Working quickly, pour syrup mixture immediately into peanut butter, stirring constantly, just until blended. Pour into prepared pan. Let cool 1 minute. Score (cut through but not to bottom of pan) into 1" squares. Cool completely.

   Cut candy with a sharp knife along scored lines. Dip candy in melted chocolate, allowing excess chocolate to drip back into pan. Cool completely on wax paper; place candy in decorative candy liners, if desired. **Yield:** 1 pound (36 pieces).

Allow the peanut butter mixture to cool 1 minute before scoring into 1" squares.

Make-Ahead Gingerbread House

As a child, Halloween was much-anticipated. I remember lugging around an orange plastic pumpkin almost as big as me door to door repeating every ghost and goblin's mantra "Trick or Treat." Dad would stand politely at the end of the sidewalk, waving and thanking each neighbor. After getting the sought-after treasure, my brother, Rhett, and I ran back to him answering his requisite, "Well, what'd ya get?"

The climax of the night, though, was arriving home, where Mom was awaiting us. (It was Mom's job to stay home to greet the other revelers.) Rhett and I would fall to the floor, pour out our candy, and methodically categorize every piece. Candy bars in this pile, lollipops in this pile, and so on. We were allowed to eat a few pieces of candy that night, but it was Mom who would get most of it.

Mom salvaged through the candy piles like a distinguishing connoisseur of confection, choosing those pieces that would be anointed the title of "gingerbread house candy"—tootsie rolls for wooden logs, candycorn for icicles, peppermint candy for windows. All would be saved for our Christmas gingerbread house. And, according to us kids, this would be the best "haul" ever for the best gingerbread house ever.

Whitney Pickering
Foods Editor, *Christmas with* Southern Living

Whitney Pickering and Natalie King reminisce over childhood traditions.

Gingerbread Men

One of my fondest memories is baking gingerbread cookies with my grandmother as a young girl. My cousin and I had been staying with my grandmother and were overjoyed at her suggestion that we help her with some Christmas baking. She patiently taught us how to roll out the dough, cut out gingerbread men, and decorate them. After baking them and adding a few more decorative touches, we delivered them to her neighbors to spread our holiday cheer. (Natalie shares her grandmother's gingerbread men recipe on page 101.)

Natalie King
Test Kitchens Staff, Oxmoor House

Words of Remembrance

When I was a little girl, I always wanted to be in the kitchen, because it was warm, and that's where my mother was. You never lose that feeling.

Dolly Parton

The World Is Her Oyster

My mom makes the best oyster dressing you ever put in your mouth. For as long as I can remember it has been the "job" of my sister and me to push the oysters into the dressing just before it goes into the oven. And, of course, we always leave three oysters out of the dressing to enjoy on a cracker with Tabasco. All three of us stand over the sink with oyster liquor dripping down our chins while we indulge in the oysters spared from the dressing.

Alyson Haynes
Senior Food Editor, *Weight Watchers* magazine

OYSTER DRESSING

Skillet Cornbread
1   (8-ounce) package seasoned breadcrumbs (we tested with Pepperidge Farm)
2   tablespoons poultry seasoning
1   tablespoon rubbed sage
1½ teaspoons salt
1¼ teaspoons pepper
4   stalks celery, thinly chopped (about 1 cup)
2   cloves garlic, minced
1   large onion, chopped
1   (1-pound) package chicken gizzards
2   stalks celery, quartered
1   medium onion, quartered
1   tablespoon poultry seasoning
½   teaspoon salt
¼   teaspoon pepper
1   (20-ounce) container chicken livers, drained
2   (12-ounce) containers fresh Select oysters
2   large eggs, lightly beaten

Crumble Skillet Cornbread into a large bowl. Add breadcrumbs and next 7 ingredients; stir well. Cover and let stand at room temperature 8 hours.

Place chicken gizzards in a large saucepan. Cover with water; add 2 stalks celery and next 4 ingredients. Bring to a boil. Reduce heat; simmer, uncovered, 20 minutes.

Add chicken livers to saucepan; simmer 15 additional minutes or until tender. Drain, reserving 3½ cups cooking liquid. Reserve gizzards and livers for giblet gravy, if desired.

Drain oysters, reserving liquid. Combine eggs, reserved cooking liquid, and reserved oyster liquid; add to cornbread mixture (dressing will be very moist).

Spoon cornbread mixture into a greased 13" x 9" x 2" baking dish. Push oysters gently and evenly into cornbread mixture. Bake dressing at 350° for 1 hour. **Yield:** 10 servings.

SKILLET CORNBREAD
3   cups self-rising cornmeal mix
2¼ cups buttermilk
⅓   cup vegetable oil
2   large eggs, lightly beaten
1   tablespoon shortening

Combine first 4 ingredients, stirring just until dry ingredients are moistened.

Place shortening in a 10" cast-iron skillet in a 450° oven for 5 minutes or until melted. Pour shortening into cornbread batter; stir well. Pour batter into hot skillet. Bake at 450° for 25 minutes or until golden. **Yield:** 6 to 8 servings.

MEALS IN A WINK

These tasty, casual entrées are adaptable, one-dish meals you can assemble quickly during these hectic days of shopping, traveling, and preparing for the season's many gatherings.

FAST-BREAK CHILI

4½ pounds ground chuck
2   (1¾-ounce) envelopes chili seasoning mix (we tested with French's)
3   (16-ounce) cans chili hot beans
3   (15-ounce) cans tomato sauce
1   cup water
½   teaspoon salt
¼   teaspoon pepper
Toppings: shredded Cheddar cheese, sour cream, chopped green onions

Brown beef in a Dutch oven, stirring until it crumbles. Drain and return to Dutch oven. Stir in chili mix and next 5 ingredients. Bring to a boil; reduce heat, and simmer, uncovered, 20 minutes. Serve with desired toppings. **Yield:** 16 cups.

FRUITED CHICKEN RAGOÛT

6   skinned and boned chicken breast halves
¾   cup all-purpose flour
1   teaspoon salt
½   teaspoon ground red pepper
¼   cup vegetable oil, divided
1   medium onion, cut into thin wedges
3   cloves garlic, minced
1   cup dried apple rings, finely chopped
½   cup dried cranberries
2   cups chicken broth
¼   teaspoon ground allspice

Place chicken breast halves between two sheets of heavy-duty plastic wrap, and flatten to ¼" thickness, using a meat mallet or rolling pin.

Combine flour, salt, and red pepper in a shallow dish; dredge chicken in mixture, shaking off excess.

Heat 2 tablespoons oil in a large skillet over medium-high heat until hot; add half of chicken, and brown on both sides. Remove from skillet, and set aside. Repeat procedure with remaining 2 tablespoons oil and chicken.

Place half of chicken in bottom of a 3½- or 4-quart electric slow cooker; top with onion, garlic, dried apple, and dried cranberries. Top with remaining chicken. Combine chicken broth and allspice; pour over chicken.

Cover and cook on HIGH setting for 2½ to 3 hours. Or cook on HIGH setting for 1 hour; reduce heat and cook on LOW 4 to 4½ hours. Serve with hot cooked rice, if desired. **Yield:** 6 servings.

SLOW COOKER LASAGNA
This recipe is so easy, you may never go back to the conventional method with boiled noodles and complicated assembly.

1   pound ground chuck
1   teaspoon dried Italian seasoning
1   (28-ounce) jar spaghetti sauce (we tested with Ragú Chunky Garden-Style)
⅓   cup water
8   lasagna noodles, uncooked
1   (4½-ounce) jar mushrooms
1   (15-ounce) carton ricotta cheese
2   cups shredded part-skim mozzarella cheese, divided

Cook beef and Italian seasoning in a large skillet over medium-high heat, stirring until beef crumbles; drain. Combine spaghetti sauce and water in a small bowl.

Place 4 uncooked noodles in bottom of a lightly greased 5-quart electric slow cooker. Layer with half each of beef mixture, spaghetti sauce mixture, and mushrooms.

Spread ricotta cheese over mushrooms. Sprinkle with 1 cup mozzarella cheese. Layer with remaining noodles, meat, sauce mixture, mushrooms, and mozzarella cheese. Cover and cook on HIGH setting 1 hour; reduce heat and cook on LOW setting 5 hours. **Yield:** 4 servings.

Slow Cooker
Lasagna

Mediterranean Frittata

MEDITERRANEAN FRITTATA

Serve this meatless main dish with crusty Italian bread.

8   pitted kalamata olives, chopped (about ¼ cup)
1   medium zucchini, cut into ½" cubes (about 2 cups)
1   sweet red pepper, diced
½   cup chopped onion
¼   cup olive oil
9   large eggs, lightly beaten
½   (4-ounce) package crumbled feta cheese (about
         ½ cup)
⅓   cup thinly sliced fresh basil
½   teaspoon salt
½   teaspoon freshly ground pepper
⅓   cup freshly grated Parmesan cheese
Garnish: fresh basil sprigs

Cook first 4 ingredients in hot oil in a 10" ovenproof skillet over medium-high heat, stirring constantly, until vegetables are tender.

Combine eggs and next 4 ingredients; pour into skillet over vegetables. Cover and cook over medium-low heat 10 to 12 minutes or until almost set. Remove from heat, and sprinkle with Parmesan cheese.

Broil 5½" from heat (with electric oven door partially opened) 2 to 3 minutes or until golden. Cut frittata into wedges; garnish, if desired. Serve warm or at room temperature. **Yield:** 6 servings.

THAI PASTA WITH TURKEY

Here, leftover turkey takes a delicious break from sandwiches.

12 ounces linguine, uncooked
½ cup canned chicken broth
3 tablespoons seasoned rice vinegar
2 tablespoons soy sauce
2 tablespoons creamy peanut butter
1 tablespoon minced fresh garlic
½ teaspoon ground ginger
½ teaspoon dried crushed red pepper
½ pound roasted turkey or chicken, coarsely chopped
⅓ cup minced fresh cilantro
¼ cup chopped roasted peanuts
Asian Salad

Cook pasta according to package directions. Keep warm.

    Meanwhile, combine broth and next 6 ingredients in a small saucepan. Cook over medium heat until mixture comes to a simmer, stirring occasionally.

    Add broth mixture to hot pasta; stir well. Add turkey and cilantro; toss gently. Sprinkle with peanuts. Serve with Asian Salad. **Yield:** 4 servings.

Asian Salad: Combine 1 (12-ounce) package coleslaw mix without dressing and ½ cup Asian-style salad dressing; toss well. Serve over fresh spinach. **Yield:** 4 servings.

COUNTRY GRITS AND SAUSAGE CASSEROLE

To punch up the flavor, use one pound of mild sausage and one pound of hot in this casserole. If you're really brave, use hot sausage exclusively!

2 pounds mild ground pork sausage
4 cups water
1¼ cups quick-cooking grits, uncooked
4 cups (1 pound) shredded sharp Cheddar cheese
1 cup milk
½ teaspoon dried thyme
⅛ teaspoon garlic powder
4 large eggs, lightly beaten
Paprika
Garnish: fresh parsley sprigs

Brown sausage in a large skillet, stirring until it crumbles. Drain well, and set aside.

    Bring water to a boil in a large saucepan, and stir in grits. Return to a boil; cover, reduce heat, and simmer

5 minutes, stirring occasionally. Remove from heat; add cheese and next 3 ingredients, stirring until cheese melts. Stir in sausage and eggs.

    Spoon mixture into a lightly greased 13" x 9" x 2" baking dish; sprinkle with paprika. Bake, uncovered, at 350° for 1 hour or until golden and heated. Let stand 5 minutes before serving. Garnish, if desired. **Yield:** 10 servings.

Make-Ahead: Prepare grits mixture as directed above, but do not bake. Cover and chill overnight. Remove from refrigerator; let stand, covered, 30 minutes. Uncover and bake as directed.

CHICKEN-PECAN QUICHE

We loved this Southern take on quiche with its Cheddar cheese, chicken, pecan topping, and savory Cheddar crust so much we gave it our highest rating.

1 cup all-purpose flour
1 cup (4 ounces) shredded sharp Cheddar cheese
¾ cup chopped pecans
½ teaspoon salt
¼ teaspoon paprika
⅓ cup vegetable oil
1 cup sour cream
½ cup chicken broth
¼ cup mayonnaise
3 large eggs, lightly beaten
2 cups finely chopped cooked chicken
½ cup (2 ounces) shredded sharp Cheddar cheese
¼ cup minced fresh onion
¼ teaspoon dried dillweed
3 drops of hot sauce
¼ cup pecan halves

Combine first 5 ingredients in a medium bowl; stir well. Add oil; stir well. Firmly press mixture on bottom and up sides of a 9" deep-dish pieplate. Bake at 350° for 12 minutes. Cool completely.

    Combine sour cream, broth, mayonnaise, and eggs; stir with a wire whisk until smooth. Stir in chicken and next 4 ingredients. Pour chicken mixture over prepared crust. Arrange pecan halves over chicken mixture. Bake at 350° for 55 minutes or until set. Let stand 10 minutes before serving. **Yield:** one 9" quiche.

Note: You can substitute turkey or a 9-ounce package of frozen diced cooked chicken for the chopped cooked chicken.

Cranberry-
Pear Salad
(page 85)

Spicy Candy
Cane
Breadsticks
(page 95)

Fast-Break Chili
(page 76)

OPEN HOUSE OPTIONS

When you want to entertain in a freewheeling fashion, an open house is the way to go. Three variations of this popular get-together— Breakfast Buffet, Appetizer Offerings, and Simple Supper— show you how to put together recipes in this book for a foolproof party.

Cranberry-Raspberry
Sangría (page 87)

Caramel-Nut
Pull-Apart
Bread (page 92)

Option #1: Breakfast Buffet

An open house in the morning? Yes! Especially if you're competing with all the other parties this season—remember Friday and Saturday nights book up quickly. This party's the perfect option for getting to know your neighbors or for entertaining close friends.

MENU SERVES 10 TO 12:
Country Grits and Sausage Casserole (page 79) or
Chicken-Pecan Quiche (page 79)

Caramel-Nut Pull-Apart Bread (page 92)

Assorted fruit platter

Overnight Bloody Marys (page 87)

Orange Juice   Coffee

Best Advice: Unless you want get up at 5:00 a.m., prepare recipes like our Country Grits and Sausage Casserole ahead of time. Do as much of the work for the entire event the day and evening before so that you can wake up refreshed to meet your guests.

Behind the Scenes: Guests will be arriving in full daylight rather than during the dark, so give some thought to your home's exterior. Hang wreaths, decorate your mailbox, wash front windows—anything to give your place its freshest face. (Find some decorating ideas for your front door on pages 8, 13, and 28.)

Recipe File: Remember, you can make the casserole ahead. Just follow the make-ahead directions on page 79. If you serve Chicken-Pecan Quiche, prepare two recipes (to serve 12). Round out the buffet with a simple fruit platter: Buy two bunches of red or green grapes, a honeydew melon, and a cantaloupe. Slice each melon, arrange slices in the middle of a platter, and surround with grape clusters.

Countdown to Any Party

Organization is the secret to effortless entertaining.

A MONTH AHEAD
- Set a date and time.
- Make out your guest list, and decide which menu you'll use. These menus serve 12 to 24, but you can double or halve each of them easily.

THREE WEEKS AHEAD
- Mail your invitations three weeks ahead—holiday schedules fill quickly.

TWO WEEKS TO GO
- Check your supply of linens and tableware, including serving dishes of different sizes and shapes (which make a more interesting buffet table). If you come up short, ask a friend or relative to lend you a few pieces. If convenience is most important to you, buy paper napkins and plastic wine glasses, plates, and utensils.

ONLY ONE MORE WEEK
- Select Christmas music to play.
- Grocery shop for nonperishable items.
- Plan timetable of the recipes you can prepare ahead.

ONE OR TWO DAYS BEFORE
- Clean your house. If you're too busy, think about hiring a cleaning crew. Or delegate specific chores to family members. You don't want to be too tired from cleaning to enjoy your guests' company.

- Arrange a centerpiece for the buffet table. Buy fresh flowers or greenery and put them in vases, or set out a few pots of seasonal bulbs in bloom. An arrangement of candles and holiday ornaments can look lovely as well and won't wilt like a floral centerpiece.
- Arrange furniture to maximize seating.
- Sideboards and dining room tables are popular locations for setting up a dinner buffet, but don't forget that you can use kitchen counters or furniture that is a similar height. Wherever you choose to set up your buffet, set out the linens and decorations, and plan exactly where you'll place each dish. Arrange plates, utensils, and serving dishes in logical order for guests to serve themselves without backtracking. Make sure that each dish has its serving utensil.
- Grocery shop for perishable items.
- Prepare recipes according to your plan.

THE BIG DAY
- Make last-minute preparations to food, and arrange in serving dishes.
- Pretend you're a guest, and walk through your front door. Think about coat storage and traffic flow—not only around the buffet table but also throughout your house.
- Are pets invited to the party? If not, find them a comfortable spot elsewhere.

Option #2: Appetizer Offerings

*A menu exclusively of finger food is your best bet if you're planning to serve
a large number of people, especially if you don't have a place to seat everyone.*

MENU SERVES 24:

Garlic-Pepper Parmesan Crisps (page 88)

Colorful Christmas Pâté with assorted crackers and baguette slices (page 87)

BLT Dippers (page 87)   Crab-Stuffed Peppers (page 88)

Prosciutto-Wrapped Shrimp (page 88)

Cranberry-Raspberry Sangría (page 87)   Assorted soft drinks

Best Advice: If you're preparing all the food yourself, select make-ahead hors d'oeuvres to avoid last-minute cooking. Running out of time? Prepare a few recipes yourself; then fill in with food purchased from the deli such as smoked salmon, sliced roast beef, or boiled peel-and-eat shrimp. Your guests will never know you didn't cook everything yourself if you transfer these items to your own serving pieces. Because meat and seafood are always popular foods at any party, offset them with substantial fillers like cheese, dips, and spreads to keep the cost down.

Behind the Scenes: Select the trays and containers you'll need; then label and arrange their positions on the table. Labels help you remember your plan if you're in a rush,

but, most importantly, they allow others to help you carry out your plan without your supervision. Also, placement of food sometimes determines what guests eat the most, so separate the more expensive items, putting at least one near the end of the buffet. Set trays that most often need replenishing close to the kitchen. If your seating area is limited, encourage guests to scatter throughout the main part of the house after they serve themselves.

Recipe File: Triple the recipe for the shrimp, and double the recipes for the dippers and stuffed peppers. The sangría recipe needs to be doubled to serve 24; instead of doubling it, though, you may want to offer a nonalcoholic punch like Sparkling Cinnamon Punch (page 87) or soft drinks.

BLT Dippers

Prosciutto-Wrapped Shrimp

Spicy Candy
Cane Breadsticks

Cranberry-
Pear Salad

Fast-Break
Chili

Option #3: Simple Supper

A casual dinner buffet offers the graciousness of a meal without the host having to serve it.
You'll have the freedom to mingle with guests and replenish food as needed. It's a great idea
if your table seating is limited and you're not expecting an overflowing house of guests.

MENU SERVES 12:

Fast-Break Chili (page 76)

Spicy Candy Cane Breadsticks (page 95)

Cranberry-Pear Salad (at right)

Best Advice: Juggling plates, cutlery, and drinks can be tricky. Tie the silverware to the cups with ribbon for easy transport (see photo on page 80), and serve the beverages from a separate table or sideboard. That way, guests can simply set their plates down and go back to retrieve their drinks.

Behind the Scenes: Serving a buffet looks effortless at the party, but it requires careful planning. To create an intimate mood, set the stage with a variety of candles and Christmas greenery. Make sure all the food is simple to serve and eat. Guests are more likely to go back for seconds when food is presented buffet-style, so provide a big pot for the chili. This will keep you from running back and forth to the kitchen all night to refill it.

Recipe File: Each guest will get 1½ cups chili. If you're expecting a hungry bunch, consider doubling the recipe. Don't worry if you've got leftovers because the chili freezes well. Doubling the breadstick recipe will give each guest one.

Cranberry-Pear Salad: Combine 3 (8-ounce) packages of lettuce, 1 cup chopped toasted walnuts, ¾ cup sweetened dried cranberries, and 3 chopped ripe red pears. Toss with an 8-ounce bottle of vinaigrette (the salad is easily divisible to serve 4 or 8).

WHET YOUR APPETITE

*You can make most of these drinks and appetizers ahead.
The rest can be assembled even as guests arrive.*

Cranberry-Raspberry
Sangria

CRANBERRY-RASPBERRY SANGRÍA

If you like a sweeter drink, add a little more sugar to your taste.

1   (48-ounce) bottle cranberry-raspberry juice cocktail
1   (750-milliliter) bottle dry, full-bodied Spanish
        red wine
2   tablespoons Grand Marnier or orange juice
¼   cup sugar
1   orange, thinly sliced
1   lemon, thinly sliced
1   cup fresh cranberries or fresh raspberries
2   cups club soda, chilled
Garnish: citrus rind curls

Combine first 4 ingredients in a large pitcher, stirring until sugar dissolves. Add fruit slices and cranberries; cover and chill at least 8 hours. Stir in club soda and ice cubes just before serving. Garnish, if desired. **Yield:** 12½ cups.

OVERNIGHT BLOODY MARYS

1   (46-ounce) can tomato juice
1   (46-ounce) can vegetable juice
1   cup lemon juice
½   cup water
2   tablespoons Worcestershire sauce
1   teaspoon salt
½   teaspoon seasoned salt
3   cups vodka
Garnish: celery stalks

Combine first 7 ingredients in a large container; stir well. Cover and chill at least 8 hours. Stir in vodka just before serving. Serve over ice. Garnish, if desired. **Yield:** 1 gallon.

SPARKLING CINNAMON PUNCH

1   cup water
½   cup sugar
½   cup red cinnamon candies
2   (2-liter) bottles raspberry-ginger ale or regular ginger
        ale, chilled
1   (46-ounce) can apple juice or apple cider, chilled

Combine first 3 ingredients in a small saucepan; bring to a boil. Reduce heat, and simmer, uncovered, 5 minutes or until candies melt, stirring occasionally. Cool completely.

Combine cinnamon mixture, ginger ale, and apple juice in a large punch bowl; stir well. **Yield:** 25 cups (about 6 quarts).

COLORFUL CHRISTMAS PÂTÉ

1   (8-ounce) package cream cheese, softened
1   (4-ounce) package feta cheese
1   cup loosely packed fresh basil leaves
1   cup loosely packed fresh parsley sprigs
¼   cup pine nuts, toasted
3   tablespoons olive oil
3   cloves garlic, divided
¾   cup oil-packed dried tomatoes, drained

Line a 2½-cup mold or bowl with plastic wrap, leaving a 1" overhang around edges. Set aside.

Beat cheeses at medium speed of an electric mixer until creamy; set aside. Combine basil and next 3 ingredients in container of an electric blender; add 2 cloves garlic. Cover and process until smooth, stopping once to scrape down sides; remove from blender, and set aside.

Combine tomatoes and remaining garlic clove in container of electric blender; process until smooth.

Spoon one-third of cream cheese mixture into prepared mold, spreading evenly; spread with basil mixture. Spoon one-third of cream cheese mixture over basil mixture, spreading evenly; spread with tomato mixture. Spread remaining cream cheese mixture over tomato mixture. Cover and chill at least 4 hours.

Unmold pâté onto a serving platter; peel off plastic wrap. Serve with baguette slices or assorted crackers. **Yield:** 2 cups.

BLT DIPPERS

The bacon filling also makes a chunky dressing for a salad.

1   cup mayonnaise
1   (8-ounce) carton sour cream
1   pound bacon, cooked and crumbled
2   large tomatoes, chopped
Belgian endive leaves

Combine mayonnaise and sour cream in a medium bowl, stirring well with a wire whisk; stir in bacon and tomato. Spoon 1 tablespoon onto individual Belgian endive leaves, or serve with Melba toast rounds. **Yield:** 4 cups.

PROSCIUTTO-WRAPPED SHRIMP

Be careful not to marinate the shrimp too long. It makes them tough.

16   unpeeled, jumbo fresh shrimp
½   cup olive oil
¼   cup vermouth
2   teaspoons dried oregano
1   teaspoon freshly ground pepper
6   cloves garlic, minced
16   (8"x 1") slices prosciutto

Peel and devein shrimp. Combine oil and next 4 ingredients in a large heavy-duty, zip-top plastic bag. Add shrimp; seal bag, and marinate in refrigerator 1 hour, turning once.

Soak 8 (6") wooden skewers in water to cover at least 30 minutes.

Remove shrimp from marinade, discarding marinade. Wrap 1 piece prosciutto around each shrimp. Thread 2 shrimp onto each skewer. Place skewers on rack of a lightly greased broiler pan. Broil 5½" from heat (with electric oven door partially opened) 7 to 9 minutes or until shrimp turn pink, turning once. **Yield:** 8 servings.

CRAB-STUFFED PEPPERS

½   pound fresh crabmeat, drained and flaked (about 2 cups)
2   green onions, finely chopped (about ¼ cup)
1   plum tomato, seeded and finely chopped
1   tablespoon minced fresh basil or parsley
½   cup mayonnaise
2   teaspoons lemon juice
½   teaspoon hot sauce
3   large red or green peppers
Fresh basil, sliced into thin strips

Combine first 4 ingredients in a medium bowl; stir in mayonnaise, lemon juice, and hot sauce. Cover and chill.

Meanwhile, cut peppers into 1½ " strips. (For bite-size pieces, cut strips in half crosswise.) Spoon crab filling onto pepper strips, and top with basil strips. **Yield:** 16 appetizer servings.

Make-Ahead: Cut peppers into strips, and store in heavy-duty, zip-top plastic bags. Prepare crabmeat mixture 8 hours ahead. For a twist, top baguette slices with the crab mixture.

CRISP POTATO WEDGES WITH CAVIAR

If caviar isn't available, minced fresh chives make an inexpensive alternative.

¼   cup plus 2 tablespoons salmon (red) caviar
2   large russet potatoes (about 1½ pounds)
1   tablespoon lemon juice
½   teaspoon salt
2   tablespoons butter or margarine
½   cup sour cream
Garnish: fresh chives

Rinse and drain caviar; place in a small bowl. Cover tightly, and chill.

Peel and shred potatoes, working quickly to prevent browning; place in a bowl. Add lemon juice and salt; toss well. Cover with heavy-duty plastic wrap, pressing directly on potato mixture. Melt butter in a 10" oven-proof nonstick skillet over medium heat. Pour potato mixture into skillet, spreading evenly to edges. Cook 4 to 5 minutes or just until edges begin to brown (do not stir). Place skillet on top baking rack in oven; bake at 450° for 30 minutes or until potato is golden and crisp on bottom.

Invert potato onto cutting board; cut into 8 wedges. Place wedges on serving plates; dollop with sour cream. Top with caviar. Garnish, if desired. **Yield:** 8 servings.

Make-Ahead: Shred potatoes a day ahead; place in cold water to cover. Cover and chill. When ready to cook, rinse potato; press between paper towels to remove excess water. Toss in lemon juice and salt. Cook over medium heat 25 minutes. Bake at 450° for 30 minutes. Rinse, drain, and chill caviar shortly before serving to retain moisture.

GARLIC-PEPPER PARMESAN CRISPS

12   ounces freshly grated Parmigiano-Reggiano cheese
2   teaspoons minced fresh garlic
1   teaspoon freshly ground pepper

Combine all ingredients in a small bowl, stirring well. Sprinkle cheese mixture into a 1½" round cookie cutter on a nonstick cookie sheet. Repeat procedure with cheese mixture, placing 16 circles on each sheet. Bake at 350° for 9 to 10 minutes or until golden. Cool slightly on baking sheets. Remove to wire racks to cool completely. Repeat procedure 5 times with remaining cheese mixture. **Yield:** 96 appetizers.

Crisp Potato Wedge
With Caviar

89

Cranberry Christmas
Tree Bread

RISING TO THE OCCASION

These impressive recipes for holiday breads start with convenience products such as hot roll mix, canned biscuits, and frozen bread dough.

CRANBERRY CHRISTMAS TREE BREAD

Not only does this recipe use a convenient frozen bread dough, it also uses purchased frosting. What a time-saver!

1½ cups fresh or frozen cranberries
¾   cup sugar
1   tablespoon fresh orange juice
1½ teaspoons grated orange rind
½   (16-ounce) package frozen bread dough, thawed
2   tablespoons butter, melted
⅓   cup chopped walnuts (optional)
¼   cup cream cheese-flavored ready-made frosting

Combine first 4 ingredients in a medium saucepan, stirring well. (Frozen berries do not have to thaw first.) Cook over medium-high heat, stirring constantly, until thickened (about 10 minutes). Set aside, and cool.

Roll dough into an 18" x 9" rectangle; brush with melted butter. Spread cranberry mixture over dough to within ½" of edges. Sprinkle with walnuts, if desired. Roll up dough, starting at long side, pressing gently to contain filling; pinch ends to seal. Cut roll into 16 equal slices (about 1⅛" thick).

On lower third of a large greased baking sheet, arrange 5 slices, cut sides up, in a row with edges touching. Form tree with additional rows of rolls, ending with 1 roll on top of tree and 1 roll on bottom for trunk.

Cover and let rise in a warm place (85°), free from drafts, 30 to 45 minutes or until doubled in bulk. Bake at 350° for 20 minutes or until lightly browned. Carefully remove from baking sheet, and cool on a wire rack.

Place frosting in a 2-cup glass measuring cup. Microwave, uncovered, at HIGH for 20 to 25 seconds or until drizzling consistency; drizzle over bread. **Yield:** 16 servings.

WHITE CHOCOLATE-MACADAMIA NUT MUFFINS

Three very different muffins are made from one basic recipe. They're all best served warm.

2½ cups biscuit and baking mix
½   cup sugar
¾   cup coarsely chopped white chocolate (we tested with Bakers Premium white chocolate)
½   cup coarsely chopped macadamia nuts
¾   cup half-and-half
3   tablespoons vegetable oil
2   teaspoons vanilla extract
1   large egg, lightly beaten

Combine baking mix and sugar in a large bowl; stir in chocolate and nuts. Make a well in center of mixture. Combine half-and-half and remaining 3 ingredients; add to dry ingredients, stirring just until dry ingredients are moistened.

Spoon into greased muffin pans, filling two-thirds full. Bake at 400° for 11 to 12 minutes or until a wooden pick inserted into center comes out clean. Remove from pans immediately. **Yield:** 1 dozen.

Hot Chocolate Muffins: Omit white chocolate and macadamia nuts. Decrease baking mix to 2¼ cups and half-and-half to ½ cup. Stir in 2 tablespoons cocoa, ¾ cup semisweet chocolate mini-morsels, ¼ cup chocolate syrup, and ¼ cup sliced almonds. Bake as directed. **Yield:** 1 dozen.

Ham and Cheese Muffins: Omit sugar, chocolate, nuts, and vanilla. Add ¾ cup diced ham (for maximum flavor, use country ham) and ¾ cup shredded sharp Cheddar cheese. Bake as directed. **Yield:** 1 dozen.

CARAMEL-NUT PULL-APART BREAD

This warm, gooey bread is best served immediately.

1   cup plus 2 tablespoons firmly packed brown sugar
1   cup chopped walnuts
¾   cup butter, melted
3   (10-ounce) cans refrigerated cinnamon-sugar biscuits
     (we tested with Pillsbury Hungry Jack)

Combine brown sugar and walnuts in a small bowl. Stir in butter. Spoon half of sugar mixture in bottom of a greased Bundt pan.

Cut each biscuit in half (use kitchen scissors for quick cutting). Place half of biscuit halves alternately over sugar mixture. Spoon remaining sugar mixture over biscuits in pan; top with remaining biscuits. Bake at 350° for 30 to 35 minutes or until browned. Turn out onto a serving platter immediately, spooning any sauce left in pan over bread. **Yield:** 12 servings.

PUMPKIN-MOLASSES MUFFINS

Molasses lends old-fashioned flavor to these moist and rich muffins.

½   cup butter or margarine, softened
¾   cup firmly packed brown sugar
1   large egg
1   cup canned pumpkin
¼   cup molasses
1¾   cups all-purpose flour
1   tablespoon baking soda
¼   teaspoon salt
¾   teaspoon ground ginger
¼   cup chopped pecans

Beat butter at medium speed of an electric mixer until creamy; gradually add brown sugar, beating well. Add egg, beating well. Add pumpkin and molasses, beating well.

Combine flour and next 3 ingredients; gradually add to pumpkin mixture, beating at medium-low just until blended. Stir in pecans. Spoon into greased muffin pans, filling three-fourths full. Bake at 375° for 20 minutes. Remove from pans immediately. **Yield:** 1 dozen.

HERBED FAN TAN DINNER ROLLS

When baked, the layers in this roll spread out to mimic a fan.

¼   butter or margarine, melted
½   teaspoon dried Italian seasoning
1   (17.4-ounce) package refrigerated loaf bread (we tested with Pillsbury Homestyle)

Combine butter and Italian seasoning, stirring well.

Roll dough into a 15" x 8" rectangle. Cut into 4 (2"-wide) lengthwise strips. Stack strips on top of each other. Cut strips crosswise into 12 equal pieces.

Place each piece, cut side up, into greased muffin pans; brush with butter mixture. Cover and let rise in a warm place (85°), free from drafts, 25 minutes or until doubled in bulk. Bake at 375° for 20 minutes or until golden. Brush with butter mixture again, if desired. **Yield:** 1 dozen.

Make-Ahead: Place dough pieces in muffin pans; brush with butter mixture. Cover and freeze. Thaw, covered, in a warm place, 2 hours or until doubled in bulk. Bake as directed.

FAN TAN STEP-BY-STEP

Stack the 15" strips on top of each other; then cut crosswise into 12 equal stacks.

Place the 12 stacks into greased muffin cups.

Herbed Fan Tan
Dinner Rolls

Sage and Onion
Cornbread

SAGE AND ONION CORNBREAD

Looking for a twist on the traditional cornbread dressing served with turkey? The onions and peppers give this cornbread moistness, and the cast-iron skillet lends a crunchy crust. The caramelized onions and fresh sage leaves make a spectacular presentation when the bread is turned out of the skillet.

½ cup butter, melted and divided
1¾ cups buttermilk self-rising cornmeal mix (we tested with Martha White)
1¼ cups milk
1 cup frozen vegetable seasoning blend*
1½ teaspoons rubbed sage
2 large eggs, lightly beaten
1 very small onion, thinly sliced
8 fresh sage leaves

Preheat oven to 425°. Place a well-seasoned 8" cast-iron skillet in hot oven 10 minutes. Add ¼ cup butter to skillet, and heat 5 additional minutes.

Combine remaining ¼ cup butter, cornmeal mix, and next 4 ingredients, stirring well with a wire whisk; let stand 2 minutes.

Arrange onion and sage leaves in bottom of hot skillet; pour batter slowly over onion and sage.

Bake at 425° for 35 to 40 minutes or until a wooden pick inserted in center comes out clean. Invert skillet over serving plate to remove bread. Cut bread into wedges to serve. **Yield:** 8 servings.

*You can substitute 1 cup chopped onion, chopped green pepper, and chopped sweet red pepper mixed together for the frozen seasoning blend.

93

Pesto Provolone
Batter Bread

PESTO PROVOLONE BATTER BREAD

You can easily substitute homemade pesto in this simple dinner bread; use about ⅓ cup.

1   (16-ounce) package hot roll mix (we tested with
       Pillsbury)
½   cup plus 2 tablespoons (2.5 ounces) shredded
       provolone cheese, divided
1¼ cups hot water (120° to 130°)
1   large egg
1   (3.5-ounce) jar pesto basil sauce (we tested with
       Alessi)
1   tablespoon pine nuts

Combine roll mix, yeast packet, and ½ cup cheese in a large mixing bowl, stirring well; add hot water and egg, beating 2 minutes at medium speed of a heavy-duty electric stand mixer. Add pesto, beating well.

Scrape dough from sides of bowl. Cover and let rise in a warm place (85°), free from drafts, 30 minutes or until doubled in bulk. Stir dough 25 strokes with a wooden spoon.

Spoon batter into a greased 2-quart round casserole; sprinkle with pine nuts.

Sprinkle batter with remaining 2 tablespoons cheese. Bake at 350° for 45 minutes or until loaf is brown. **Yield:** 10 servings.

SPICY CANDY CANE BREADSTICKS

These are perfect companions for gumbo, stew, or chili. They're shaped like candy canes, but they're spicy hot rather than sweet!

1   (11-ounce) can refrigerated breadstick dough
1   large egg, lightly beaten
2   tablespoons paprika
2   tablespoons seasoned pepper blend* (we tested with McCormick)

Separate breadsticks; working with two at a time, roll each breadstick into a 20" rope. Brush ropes with egg. Twist ropes together, pinching ends to seal. Repeat with remaining breadsticks.

Combine paprika and pepper blend; spread mixture on a paper plate. Roll breadsticks in pepper mixture, pressing gently to coat. (Wash hands between rolling each bread-stick, if necessary.)

Place breadsticks on a greased baking sheet, curving top of breadstick to form a candy cane. Bake at 375° for 10 minutes. **Yield:** 6 servings.

*If you can't find seasoned pepper blend, combine equal portions of cracked pepper, sweet red pepper flakes, and salt.

CHIVE 'N' CHEDDAR DROP BISCUITS

These biscuits may remind you of a famous seafood restaurant's biscuits.

3   cups biscuit and baking mix
1   cup (4 ounces) finely shredded sharp Cheddar cheese
1   tablespoon chopped fresh or dried chives
½   teaspoon garlic powder
1¼ cups milk
½   cup sour cream
3   tablespoons butter, melted

Combine first 4 ingredients in a large bowl; make a well in center of mixture.

Combine milk and sour cream; add to dry ingredients, stirring just until dry ingredients are moistened.

Drop by ¼ cupfuls onto a lightly greased baking sheet; brush with butter. Bake at 425° for 8 to 10 minutes or until golden. **Yield:** 16 biscuits.

EGGNOG TEA BREAD

Use your extra eggnog to make this sweet bread that makes enough little loaves for you and three friends.

1   (16-ounce) package pound cake mix (we tested with Betty Crocker)
¾   cup refrigerated eggnog
½   teaspoon ground nutmeg
2   large eggs
1   cup sifted powdered sugar
1   tablespoon refrigerated eggnog

Combine first 4 ingredients in a large mixing bowl; beat at medium speed of an electric mixer 3 minutes. Pour batter into 4 greased 6" x 3" x 2" loafpans. Bake at 350° for 30 minutes or until a wooden pick inserted in center comes out clean. Remove from pans; cool on wire racks.

Combine powdered sugar and 1 tablespoon eggnog, stirring well; drizzle over bread. **Yield:** 4 loaves.

LEMON-SWIRLED GINGERBREAD

The traditional pairing of gingerbread and lemon curd takes a surprising turn in this recipe—the lemon curd is baked right in.

2   (3-ounce) packages cream cheese, softened
¼   cup sugar
1   large egg
½   cup lemon curd
1   (10-ounce) package gingerbread mix (we tested with Betty Crocker)
2   teaspoons lemon-flavored powdered sugar or regular powdered sugar

Place cream cheese in a medium mixing bowl; beat at medium speed of an electric mixer until smooth. Gradually add ¼ cup sugar, beating well. Add egg, beating just until blended. Fold in lemon curd.

Prepare gingerbread batter according to package directions. Pour half of batter into a greased 8" square pan. Dollop lemon mixture over batter; pour remaining batter over lemon mixture. Swirl a knife through batter, touching bottom of pan and swirling to bring some lemon mixture to top of cake. Bake at 350° for 35 minutes or until knife inserted in center comes out clean. Cool in pan on a wire rack. Sift powdered sugar over cake. **Yield:** 9 servings.

HEIRLOOM COOKIES

*What ever happened to macaroons, lizzies, and shortbread?
We've preserved some timeless recipes in this treasury of treats from
grandmother's day to pass on to the next generation.*

Melt-in-Your-Mouth
Iced Sugar Cookies

MELT-IN-YOUR-MOUTH ICED SUGAR COOKIES

1 cup butter, softened
1½ cups sugar
1 large egg
3 cups all-purpose flour
½ teaspoon baking soda
½ teaspoon salt
1 teaspoon cream of tartar
2 teaspoons vanilla extract
Royal Icing
Assorted colors paste food coloring
Decorator sprinkles

Beat butter at medium speed of an electric mixer 2 minutes or until creamy. Gradually add sugar, beating well. Add egg, and beat well. Combine flour and next 3 ingredients. Add to butter mixture, beating at low speed just until blended. Stir in vanilla.

Roll dough to ¼" thickness on a lightly floured surface. Cut with decorative 3" cookie cutters. Place 1" apart on ungreased cookie sheets. Bake at 350° for 9 minutes. Cool completely on wire racks.

Spoon about ⅔ cup white Royal Icing into a decorating bag fitted with decorating tip #3 (small round tip). Pipe white icing to outline cookies and to outline detail desired inside cookies (see Photo **1**).

Divide remaining Royal Icing into a separate bowl for each color desired; color as desired with paste food coloring. Slowly stir just enough water into each bowl of icing to make "flow-in icing" that is still thick but flows into a smooth surface after stirring. (Add water a little at a time; if flow-in icing is too watery, it may not dry properly and may run under outline into another color area.)

Fill decorating bags (using no tips) about half full of flow-in icing. Snip off small tip of cone. Pipe desired colors of icing to cover areas between the Royal Icing outline (see Photo **2**); spread icing into corners and hard-to-reach areas using a wooden pick, as necessary (see Photo **3**). Add flow-in icing 1 color at a time, allowing icing to dry before changing colors. Avoid using excess icing, or it will spill over into another color area. If air bubbles form in icing, use a sterilized straight pin to remove them. Decorate with assorted candies and decorator sprinkles while icing is still wet. **Yield:** 3½ dozen.

ROYAL ICING

This icing dries very quickly, so keep it covered at all times with a damp cloth to help keep it moist.

3 large egg whites
1 (16-ounce) package powdered sugar, sifted and divided
½ teaspoon cream of tartar

Combine egg whites, 1 cup powdered sugar, and cream of tartar in top of a double boiler. Place over simmering water. Cook, stirring constantly with a wire whisk, 9 minutes or until mixture reaches 160°. Remove from heat. Transfer to a large mixing bowl, and add remaining powdered sugar.

Beat at high speed of an electric mixer 5 to 8 minutes or until stiff peaks form. **Yield:** 2 cups.

1. Pipe Royal Icing to outline cookies and add detail inside cookies as desired.

2. Pipe desired colors of flow-in icing to cover areas within the white icing outline.

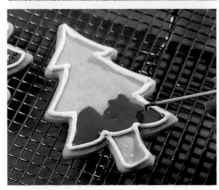

3. Use a wooden pick to spread icing into corners and hard-to-reach areas as needed. Sprinkle on decorator candies as desired while icing is still wet.

OATMEAL-FRUITCAKE LIZZIES

Fruit and nuts contribute chewy and crunchy surprises to this soft cookie that's ideal for a Christmas cookie swap.

1	cup shortening
1	cup sugar
1	cup firmly packed brown sugar
2	large eggs
1	teaspoon almond extract
1	teaspoon vanilla extract
2	cups all-purpose flour
1	teaspoon baking powder
1	teaspoon baking soda
1	teaspoon salt
2	cups regular oats, uncooked
1	cup chopped pecans
¾	cup golden raisins
¾	cup chopped red and green candied cherries
¾	cup chopped candied pineapple

Beat shortening at medium speed of an electric mixer until creamy; gradually add sugars, beating well. Add eggs and flavorings; beat well.

Combine flour and next 4 ingredients; gradually add to shortening mixture, beating well. Stir in pecans and remaining ingredients.

Drop dough by heaping tablespoonfuls onto lightly greased cookie sheets. Bake at 350° for 10 minutes or until golden. Remove to wire racks, and cool completely. **Yield:** 7½ dozen.

MACAROON TARTLETS

The buttery crust of these mini tarts encases a soft almond paste filling.

1	cup butter, softened
1	cup sugar, divided
3	large eggs, divided
1	teaspoon vanilla extract
2	cups all-purpose flour
1	pound almond paste
½	teaspoon almond extract
½	cup slivered almonds

Beat butter at medium speed of an electric mixer until creamy; gradually add ½ cup sugar, beating well. Add 1 egg and vanilla; beat well. Gradually add flour; beat well.

Shape dough into 48 (1") balls; press balls into lightly greased miniature (1¾") muffin pans, pressing evenly into bottom and up sides. Set aside.

Beat almond paste at medium speed until creamy; gradually add remaining ½ cup sugar, beating well.

Add almond extract and remaining 2 eggs, beating well. Spoon mixture into prepared shells. Top each tartlet with 3 slivered almonds. Bake at 325° for 25 minutes or until golden. Cool in pans on wire racks 10 minutes; remove to wire racks, and cool completely. **Yield:** 4 dozen.

ULTIMATE CHOCOLATE COMFORT COOKIES

Chock-full of all your favorites—chocolate chips, pecans, even marshmallow—these cookies offer something to everyone!

1	cup unsalted butter, softened
1	(3-ounce) package cream cheese, softened
1	cup sugar
1	large egg
2	(1-ounce) squares unsweetened chocolate, melted and cooled
2	tablespoons milk
1½	teaspoons vanilla extract
2	cups plus 2 tablespoons all-purpose flour
½	teaspoon baking powder
½	teaspoon salt
¼	cup Dutch process cocoa or regular cocoa
1	cup marshmallow cream
1	cup chopped pecans
1	(11-ounce) package semisweet chocolate mega-morsels or white chocolate morsels (2 cups)
½	cup sweetened dried cranberries (we tested with Craisins)

Beat butter and cream cheese at medium speed of an electric mixer until creamy; gradually add sugar, beating well. Add egg, beating well. Add melted chocolate, milk, and vanilla; beat well.

Combine flour and next 3 ingredients; add to butter mixture, beating well. Stir in marshmallow cream and remaining ingredients, mixing well.

Drop dough by heaping tablespoonfuls onto lightly greased cookie sheets. Bake at 325° for 13 minutes or until done. Cool 1 minute on cookie sheets; remove to wire racks and cool completely. **Yield:** 4 dozen.

Peanut Butter
Fingers

Kissy
Cookies

Chunky Peanut
Butter Cookies

CHUNKY PEANUT BUTTER COOKIES

Peanut butter and wheat germ lace this flavorful cookie with rich nutrients.

1   cup extra-crunchy peanut butter
¾   cup firmly packed brown sugar
½   cup butter, softened
¼   cup honey
½   teaspoon vanilla extract
1   large egg
1½   cups all-purpose flour
½   teaspoon baking soda
½   teaspoon salt
½   cup wheat germ

Beat first 6 ingredients at medium speed of an electric mixer until creamy. Combine flour and remaining 3 ingredients. Gradually add to butter mixture, beating well.

Shape dough into 1" balls. Place 2" apart on ungreased cookie sheets. Flatten cookie balls with the back of a fork, forming a crisscross pattern. Bake at 325° for 12 minutes or until lightly browned. Cool 1 minute on cookie sheets; remove to wire racks, and cool completely. **Yield:** 4 dozen.

Kissy Cookies: Shape cookies as directed, but do not flatten with a fork. Place a chocolate kiss in each cookie while it cools on cookie sheet. Remove to wire racks to cool.

Peanut Butter Fingers: Roll 1" balls of dough into 2½" logs. Bake as directed. When logs are cool, dip 1 end of each cookie into 1½ cups melted semisweet chocolate morsels. Return cookies to wire racks, and let stand until chocolate is firm.

Note: A teaspoon measure gives you enough dough to shape into a 1" ball or a 2½" x ¾" log.

Springerle

SPRINGERLE

An intricately carved wooden mold breathes life into the traditional anise-flavored cookie dough of Germany's springerle. Springerle molds and rolling pins usually picture a theme, from nature to religion. You can find a source for this mold on page 154.

3   large eggs
2   cups sugar
2   teaspoons grated lemon rind
½   teaspoon anise extract
2¾ cups all-purpose flour
¼   teaspoon baking powder
Vegetable cooking spray

Beat eggs at medium speed of an electric mixer until pale (5 minutes). Gradually add sugar, and beat 5 additional minutes. Add lemon rind and anise extract; beat well.

Combine flour and baking powder; add to egg mixture, beating well. Cover and chill dough at least 3 hours.

Let dough stand at room temperature for 15 minutes; divide into thirds. Place 1 portion of dough on a floured surface; roll to ¼" thickness. Lightly spray mold with cooking spray. Place dough over mold; press firmly and evenly to imprint dough. Trim excess dough around rectangle. Invert onto a parchment paper-lined wire rack on a baking sheet. Repeat procedure with remaining dough.

Let cookies stand, uncovered, in a cool, dry place 1 hour to set design. (Cookies should appear slightly crusted.)

Bake at 225° for 2½ hours or until light yellow, but not golden. Cool completely on rack. Carefully remove from parchment paper. **Yield:** 3 cookies.

Lemon Springerle: Substitute lemon extract for anise extract.

ROSEMARY SHORTBREAD

Fresh rosemary updates basic but timeless shortbread.

1   cup butter, softened
¾   cup sifted powdered sugar
¼   cup cornstarch
1¾ cups all-purpose flour
1   tablespoon minced fresh rosemary

Beat butter at medium speed of an electric mixer until creamy; gradually add powdered sugar and cornstarch, beating well. Stir in flour and rosemary. (Dough will be stiff.)

Divide dough in half. Shape 1 portion of dough into a 6½" circle on an ungreased cookie sheet. Crimp edges with a fork. Cut dough into 8 wedges (do not separate). Repeat procedure with remaining dough. Cover and chill 1 hour.

Bake at 300° for 30 minutes or until done. Cool on cookie sheet 5 minutes. Remove shortbread wedges to a wire rack, and cool completely. **Yield:** 16 shortbread wedges.

GINGERBREAD MEN

A few decorations are simple enough for little helping hands. Reroll the dough to use every scrap.

1   cup shortening
1   cup sugar
1   cup molasses
2   tablespoons white vinegar
1   large egg
5   cups all-purpose flour
1½   teaspoons baking soda
½   teaspoon salt
3   teaspoons ground ginger
1   teaspoon ground cloves
1   teaspoon ground cinnamon
Currants
Red cinnamon candies

Beat shortening at medium speed of an electric mixer until creamy; gradually add sugar, beating well. Add molasses, vinegar, and egg; beat well.

Combine flour and next 5 ingredients; gradually add to shortening mixture, beating well. Shape dough into a ball; wrap in plastic wrap, and chill 8 hours.

Divide dough in half. Work with 1 portion of dough at a time, storing remainder in refrigerator. Roll each portion of dough to ⅛" thickness on a well-floured surface. Cut with a 4" gingerbread man cookie cutter; place on ungreased cookie sheets, using a floured spatula to lift cookies from work surface. Press currants into dough to form eyes, nose, and mouth. Press 3 cinnamon candies into dough for buttons.

Bake at 375° for 7 minutes or until lightly browned. Cool on cookie sheets 2 minutes; remove to wire racks, and cool completely. **Yield:** about 4 dozen.

PEPPERMINT COOKIE CANES

½ cup butter, softened
½ cup butter-flavored shortening or regular shortening
1½ cups sugar
1 large egg
1½ teaspoons peppermint extract
½ teaspoon vanilla extract
3½ cups sifted cake flour
1½ teaspoons baking powder
¼ teaspoon salt
¾ teaspoon red paste food coloring

Beat butter and shortening at medium speed of an electric mixer until creamy; gradually add sugar, beating well. Add egg, beating well. Stir in flavorings. Combine flour, baking powder, and salt; add to butter mixture, beating well. Remove half of dough from bowl. Add food coloring to dough in bowl, and mix until color is evenly distributed.

Working with half of each dough at a time, shape plain dough by teaspoonfuls into 4" ropes. (Cover remaining dough to prevent drying.) Repeat shaping with red dough. Place 1 red rope and 1 plain rope side by side; carefully twist together. Roll twisted ropes into 1 smooth rope; shape rope into a cane, and twist as needed to complete stripe design. Repeat with remaining dough. Chill 15 minutes.

Place cookie canes on ungreased cookie sheets. Bake at 375° for 8 minutes or just until cookies begin to brown.

Cool slightly; carefully remove cookies to wire racks, using a wide spatula, and cool completely. **Yield:** about 4 dozen.

PECAN BISCOTTI

1¾ cups all-purpose flour
1¼ teaspoons baking powder
¼ teaspoon salt
½ cup yellow cornmeal
1 cup finely chopped pecans
2 large eggs, lightly beaten
¾ cup sugar
½ cup vegetable oil
Dash of almond extract or vanilla extract

Combine first 5 ingredients in a large bowl. Combine eggs and remaining 3 ingredients; gradually add to flour mixture, stirring just until dry ingredients are moistened.

Place dough on a lightly floured surface; divide in half. With lightly floured hands, shape each half into a 12" x 1¼" log. Place logs 3" apart on a lightly greased baking sheet. Bake at 350° for 25 minutes; cool 10 minutes.

Cut each log crosswise into ¾"-thick slices, using a serrated knife. Place slices, cut side down, on ungreased baking sheets.

Bake at 350° for 12 minutes, turning cookies once. Remove to wire racks, and cool completely. **Yield:** 2 dozen.

SMOOTH AS A CANDY CANE

1. Place 1 red rope and 1 plain rope side by side, and carefully twist together.

2. Roll twisted ropes into 1 smooth rope, and shape rope into a cane.

DOUBLE-FROSTED BOURBON BROWNIES

¾ cup all-purpose flour
¼ teaspoon baking soda
¼ teaspoon salt
½ cup sugar
⅓ cup shortening
2 tablespoons water
1 (6-ounce) package semisweet chocolate morsels
1 teaspoon vanilla extract
2 large eggs
1 cup chopped walnuts
¼ cup bourbon
White Frosting
Chocolate Glaze

Combine first 3 ingredients, stirring well. Set aside.

Combine sugar, shortening, and water in a medium saucepan. Bring to a boil over medium heat, stirring constantly; remove from heat. Add chocolate morsels and vanilla, stirring until smooth.

Add eggs, one at a time, stirring after each addition. Add flour mixture and walnuts; stir well.

Spoon into a greased 9" square pan. Bake at 325° for 30 minutes or until a wooden pick inserted in center comes out clean.

Sprinkle bourbon evenly over warm brownies. Cool completely in pan on a wire rack. Spread White Frosting over uncut brownies. Pour warm Chocolate Glaze over frosting. Let stand until set. Cut into squares. **Yield:** 2½ dozen.

WHITE FROSTING

½ cup butter or margarine, softened
1 teaspoon vanilla extract
2 cups sifted powdered sugar

Combine butter and vanilla in a large mixing bowl; beat at medium speed of an electric mixer until creamy. Gradually add powdered sugar, beating until smooth. **Yield:** 1¼ cups.

CHOCOLATE GLAZE

1 (6-ounce) package semisweet chocolate morsels
1 tablespoon shortening

Combine chocolate morsels and shortening in top of a double boiler; bring water to a boil. Reduce heat to low; heat until chocolate morsels melt, stirring occasionally. **Yield:** ½ cup.

CHOCOLATE-ORANGE SWIRLS
Freshly grated rind accentuates the orange flavor in these memorable cookies.

1 cup butter, softened
1 cup sugar
1 large egg
1 teaspoon vanilla extract
3 cups all-purpose flour
1½ teaspoons baking powder
¼ teaspoon salt
1 teaspoon grated orange rind
1½ teaspoons orange extract
2 (1-ounce) squares semisweet chocolate, melted and cooled

Beat butter at medium speed of an electric mixer until creamy; gradually add sugar, beating well. Add egg and vanilla; beat well.

Combine flour, baking powder, and salt; stir well. Add flour mixture to butter mixture, beating at low speed.

Remove half of dough from bowl. Add orange rind and orange extract to dough in bowl, and mix well. Remove orange dough from mixing bowl, and set aside. Return plain dough to mixing bowl; add melted chocolate, beating well. Cover and chill both portions of dough 1 hour.

Roll each half of dough to a 15" x 8" rectangle on floured wax paper. Place orange dough on top of chocolate dough; peel off top wax paper. Tightly roll dough, jellyroll fashion, starting at short side and peeling wax paper from dough while rolling. Cover and chill 1 hour.

Slice dough into ¼" slices; place on ungreased cookie sheets. Bake at 350° for 10 to 12 minutes. Remove to wire racks to cool. **Yield:** 2½ dozen.

Chocolate-Cherry Swirls: Substitute ½ cup drained, minced maraschino cherries for orange rind and orange extract. Add 3 tablespoons all-purpose flour to cherry dough if it is too soft. **Yield:** 2½ dozen.

Note: To prevent flat-sided cookies, turn dough rolls halfway through the second chilling time. Dental floss makes cutting the dough easier.

SWEETS EXPRESS

*Convenience products come to the rescue once again, this time
as the main ingredients for delicious, uncomplicated desserts.*

Ambrosia
Trifle

AMBROSIA TRIFLE

1   (5.1-ounce) package vanilla instant pudding mix
3   cups milk
1   (8-ounce) container sour cream
2   tablespoons frozen orange juice concentrate, thawed
1   (28.2-ounce) package frozen golden pineapple coconut cake, partially thawed (we tested with Pepperidge Farm)
1   (15-ounce) can mandarin orange segments, drained
1½ cups frozen whipped topping, thawed
Garnishes: shredded coconut, stemmed maraschino cherries

Combine first 4 ingredients in a large bowl; beat at low speed of an electric mixer 2 minutes or until thickened.

Spoon one-third of pudding into a 3-quart trifle bowl. Cut coconut cake in half lengthwise. Cut cake halves crosswise into ½" slices. Arrange one-third of cake slices in a single layer over pudding. Arrange one-third of mandarin orange segments over cake. Arrange half of remaining cake slices over orange segments.

Cover cake with half of remaining pudding; top with remaining cake slices and half of remaining orange segments. Top with remaining pudding and orange segments. Mound whipped topping over trifle. Garnish, if desired. Cover and chill several hours. **Yield:** 12 to 14 servings.

PEANUTTY CANDY BAR BROWNIES

These brownies have a gooey center when served warm. The longer they cool, the firmer the candy bar center becomes.

1   (21-ounce) package fudge brownie mix (we tested with Duncan Hines Chewy Fudge Brownie Mix)
¼   cup vegetable oil
½   cup creamy peanut butter
3   (7-ounce) peanuts in milk chocolate candy bars (we tested with Mr. Goodbar)

Prepare brownie mix batter according to package directions, using ¼ cup oil instead of ½ cup as package directs. Stir peanut butter into batter. Spread half of brownie batter into an ungreased 13" x 9" x 2" baking pan. Place whole candy bars across batter. Spread remaining batter over candy bars.

Bake at 350° for 29 minutes. Cool completely on a wire rack. Cut into squares. **Yield:** 3 dozen.

CHOCOLATE CHIP POUND CAKE

1   (18.25-ounce) package yellow cake mix (without pudding)
1   (5.9-ounce) package chocolate instant pudding mix
½   cup sugar
⅔   cup water
¾   cup vegetable oil
1   (8-ounce) container sour cream
4   large eggs
6   ounces semisweet chocolate mini-morsels
Powdered sugar

Beat first 5 ingredients in a large mixing bowl at medium speed of an electric mixer about 2 minutes or until creamy; add sour cream, mixing well. Add eggs, one at a time, mixing at low speed just until blended after each addition. Stir in chocolate morsels. Pour batter into a greased and floured 10" tube or Bundt pan.

Bake at 350° for 1 hour or until a wooden pick inserted in center comes out clean. Cool in pan on wire rack 10 minutes; remove from pan, and cool completely on a wire rack. Sprinkle with powdered sugar before serving. **Yield:** 1 (10") cake.

MOCHA DESSERT SQUARES
This is the perfect dessert for a potluck or church supper.

2   cups whipping cream
3   tablespoons chocolate sauce
1   tablespoon instant coffee granules
1   teaspoon vanilla extract
¾   cup sifted powdered sugar
27 graham cracker squares
Garnish: chocolate sauce

Place whipping cream in a small bowl. Add 3 tablespoons chocolate sauce, coffee granules, and vanilla, stirring until granules dissolve. Beat whipping cream mixture at medium speed of an electric mixer until foamy; gradually add powdered sugar, beating until soft peaks form.

Place 9 graham cracker squares in an 8" square pan. Spread one-third of cream mixture over crackers. Repeat layers twice with remaining ingredients. Cover and chill at least 8 hours. Garnish, if desired. **Yield:** 9 servings.

UPSIDE-DOWN DATE PUDDING

1	cup whole pitted dates, chopped
1	cup boiling water
½	cup sugar
2	cups firmly packed brown sugar, divided
3	tablespoons butter, divided
1	large egg
1½	cups all-purpose flour
1	teaspoon baking soda
½	teaspoon baking powder
½	teaspoon salt
1	cup chopped walnuts
1½	cups boiling water
	Sweetened whipped cream

Combine dates and 1 cup boiling water in a small bowl; set aside.

Combine ½ cup sugar, ½ cup brown sugar, 2 tablespoons butter, and egg in a large mixing bowl; beat at medium speed of an electric mixer until blended.

Combine flour and next 3 ingredients; stir well. Add to sugar mixture, beating well. (Mixture will be crumbly.) Stir in nuts and cooled date mixture.

Spoon batter into a lightly greased 13" x 9" x 2" pan. Combine remaining 1½ cups brown sugar, 1½ cups boiling water, and remaining 1 tablespoon butter, stirring mixture well.

Pour brown sugar mixture evenly over batter. Bake at 375° for 35 to 40 minutes. Serve warm with whipped cream. **Yield:** 12 servings.

Upside-Down Date Pudding

Toffee Crunch Ice Cream Bowl

TOFFEE CRUNCH ICE CREAM BOWLS

Try your own combination of ice cream flavors and toppings for endless variations of this quick, yet showy, dessert.

2   cups coffee ice cream
3   (1.4-ounce) English toffee-flavored candy bars, crushed (we tested with Heath)
4   waffle cone bowls
Chocolate ice cream topping

Scoop ice cream into 4 balls; freeze until firm. Roll ice cream balls in crushed toffee bars; freeze until firm.

To serve, place ice cream balls in waffle bowls. Drizzle topping over ice cream. **Yield:** 4 servings.

ELEPHANT EARS

1   cup sugar
¼   cup ground cinnamon
1   (10-ounce) can cinnamon rolls (we tested with Pillsbury)

Combine sugar and cinnamon in a small bowl. Remove rolls from can; set icing aside. Sprinkle rolls with sugar mixture, and roll each to a 6" round. Sprinkle rolls with sugar mixture again.

Place rolls on lightly greased cookie sheets. Bake at 375° for 7 minutes. Cool slightly on cookie sheets; drizzle icing over hot rolls, if desired. **Yield:** 8 servings.

GUEST STARS

A rich dessert can be the crowning moment of your holiday dinner. Why not spend a little more time this season preparing one of these spectacular finales?

BÛCHE DE NOËL

4   large eggs, separated
⅔   cup sugar, divided
2   tablespoons water
1   teaspoon vanilla extract
½   cup ground pistachios
½   cup sifted cake flour
3   tablespoons cocoa
½   teaspoon cream of tartar
Dash of salt
2   to 3 tablespoons powdered sugar
Rich Chocolate Buttercream
¼   cup finely chopped pistachios
Garnishes: Meringue Mushrooms, bay leaves, crab apples

Grease bottom and sides of a 15" x 10" x 1" jellyroll pan; line bottom with wax paper. Grease and flour wax paper.

Beat egg yolks at high speed of an electric mixer 5 minutes or until thick and pale. Gradually add ⅓ cup sugar, beating well. Add water and vanilla. Fold in ½ cup ground pistachios. Gradually fold in cake flour and cocoa.

Beat egg whites at high speed until foamy. Add cream of tartar and salt; beat until soft peaks form. Add remaining ⅓ cup sugar, 1 tablespoon at a time, beating until stiff peaks form. Fold into yolk mixture. Spread into pan. Bake at 375° for 10 minutes or until top springs back when touched.

Sift powdered sugar in a 15" x 10" rectangle on a cloth towel. When cake is done, immediately loosen from sides of pan, and turn out onto sugared towel. Peel off wax paper. Starting at narrow end, roll up cake and towel together; cool completely on a wire rack, seam side down.

Unroll cake; remove towel. Spread cake with half of Rich Chocolate Buttercream; carefully reroll. Cover and chill. Cut a 1" thick diagonal slice from 1 end of cake roll. Place cake roll on a serving plate, seam side down; position cut piece on top of cake to resemble a knot. Spread remaining buttercream over cake.

Score frosting with the tines of a fork to resemble tree bark. Top cake with chopped pistachios for moss. Garnish sides of cake with Meringue Mushrooms, bay leaves, and crab apples. **Yield:** 10 servings.

RICH CHOCOLATE BUTTERCREAM

2   (1-ounce) squares unsweetened chocolate
2   (1-ounce) squares semisweet chocolate
1   cup butter or margarine, softened
4   cups sifted powdered sugar
¼   cup cocoa
¼   cup milk
2   teaspoons vanilla extract

Place chocolate in top of a double boiler; bring water to a boil. Reduce heat to low; cook until chocolate melts, stirring often. Remove from heat.

Beat butter at medium speed of an electric mixer until creamy. Add chocolate, powdered sugar, and remaining ingredients; beat until spreading consistency. **Yield:** 3¾ cups.

MERINGUE MUSHROOMS

3   egg whites
¼   teaspoon cream of tartar
¼   teaspoon vanilla extract
¼   teaspoon almond extract
⅛   teaspoon salt
½   cup superfine sugar
½   cup semisweet chocolate morsels, melted
2   teaspoons ground cinnamon or cocoa

Combine first 5 ingredients; beat at high speed of an electric mixer until foamy. Add sugar, 1 tablespoon at a time, beating until stiff peaks form and sugar dissolves (2 to 4 minutes).

Spoon mixture into a decorating bag fitted with a large round tip. Pipe 32 (1¼"-wide) mounds to resemble mushroom caps and 32 (1"-tall) columns to resemble stems onto a parchment paper-lined baking sheet.

Bake at 200° for 1 hour and 30 minutes; turn oven off. Let meringues stand in closed oven 2 hours.

Spread a thin layer of melted chocolate on flat side of caps. Trim rounded end of stems to make flat; press against chocolate to attach stems to caps. Sprinkle caps lightly with cinnamon or cocoa. **Yield:** 32 mushrooms.

CHEESECAKE SAMPLER

This rich, dense New York-style cheesecake received our test kitchens' highest rating—even without any toppings. Pick from one or all of our toppings that follow the main recipe.

2   cups graham cracker crumbs
½   cup butter or margarine, melted
2   tablespoons sugar
4   (8-ounce) packages cream cheese, softened
1¾   cups sugar
7   large eggs
3   (8-ounce) cartons sour cream
1   tablespoon vanilla extract
Cheesecake Toppings

Combine first 3 ingredients; stir well. Press mixture firmly onto bottom and up sides of a lightly greased 9" springform pan. Chill thoroughly.

Beat cream cheese at high speed of a heavy-duty electric mixer until fluffy. Gradually add 1¾ cups sugar, beating well. Add eggs, one at a time, beating well after each addition. Add sour cream and vanilla; beat at low speed until smooth. Pour into prepared pan. Bake at 300° for 1 hour and 25 minutes. Turn off oven, and leave cheesecake in oven 4 hours. (Do not open oven door.)

Remove from oven; cool completely on wire rack. Cover and chill 8 hours. Remove sides of springform pan; transfer cheesecake to a serving platter. Cut into 8 wedges; top each slice with desired Cheesecake Toppings. **Yield:** 8 servings.

CHEESECAKE TOPPINGS *(pictured clockwise from top)*

Orange Cheesecake: Brush orange marmalade evenly over slice. Cut candied orange slices in halves, thirds, and quarters. Arrange orange segments over slice.

Black-and-White Cheesecake: Spoon one can each ready-made chocolate and cream cheese frostings into separate microwave-safe bowls. Microwave each at HIGH 20 seconds or just until soft and pipeable. Spoon frostings into separate heavy-duty, zip-top plastic bags. Seal; snip a tiny hole in the corner of each bag. Pipe chocolate frosting in a zigzag fashion over the slice. Pipe cream cheese frosting over chocolate frosting in the opposite direction. Pipe additional chocolate frosting over cream cheese frosting. Place chocolate-covered coffee beans on crust edge, using chocolate frosting to secure in place.

Coconut Cheesecake: Spoon one can ready-made cream cheese frosting into a microwave-safe bowl. Microwave on HIGH for 40 seconds or until melted and pourable. Pour over slice; sprinkle with grated fresh or frozen coconut.

Walnut Cheesecake: Spoon walnuts-in-syrup ice cream topping over slice. (We tested with Smuckers.)

Peppermint Cheesecake: Spoon one can ready-made cream cheese frosting into a microwave-safe bowl. Microwave at HIGH for 30 seconds or until almost melted and stirrable. Combine frosting and crushed peppermint candy; stir well. Spread over slice. Place whole pillow-shaped peppermint candies around crust edge.

Raspberry Cheesecake: Brush melted seedless raspberry jam over slice. Arrange fresh raspberries over slice; brush lightly with additional melted jam.

Café au Lait Cheesecake: Spoon sweetened whipped cream or thawed frozen whipped topping into a decorating bag fitted with a large star tip. Pipe rosettes over slice, and sprinkle evenly with ground cinnamon. Place a pirouline cookie on the crust edge of slice.

Holly Cheesecake: Pipe green cake decorating gel in shape of holly leaves over slice. Arrange 3 red candy-coated chocolate-covered peanuts at top of leaves.

Cheesecake Sampler

SPICED STEAMED PUDDING WITH MAPLE SAUCE

This moist, golden pudding—lavishly garnished with fruits, nuts, and spices of the season—will make a perfect finale to your elegant holiday meal.

2   cups all-purpose flour
1½   teaspoons baking powder
1½   teaspoons ground cinnamon
½   teaspoon ground ginger
½   teaspoon ground nutmeg
¼   teaspoon ground cloves
¾   cup butter, softened
1¾   cups firmly packed brown sugar
2   large eggs
1¼   cups canned pumpkin
¾   cup chopped pecans, toasted
Garnishes: cranberries, walnuts, almonds, pecans,
         kumquats, small lady apples, cinnamon sticks
Maple Sauce

Grease a pudding mold (at least 7 cups, but up to 10 cups will work). Set aside. Combine first 6 ingredients, stirring well with a wire whisk; set aside.

Beat butter at medium speed of an electric mixer until creamy; gradually add sugar, beating well. Add eggs, one at a time, beating after each addition. Mix in pumpkin and pecans. Gradually add flour mixture; mix just until blended.

Pour mixture into prepared mold; cover with lid. Place mold on a rack in a Dutch oven. Add boiling water to Dutch oven to halfway up mold. Bring water to a boil; cover, reduce heat, and simmer 1 hour and 15 minutes or until a wooden pick inserted in center comes out clean.

Remove mold from Dutch oven; let stand, uncovered, 15 minutes. Remove pudding from mold; garnish, if desired. Serve warm with Maple Sauce. **Yield:** 12 servings.

MAPLE SAUCE
You can make this slightly sweet sauce up to one day ahead and reheat it over low heat. Do not boil.

6   large egg yolks
¼   cup maple-flavored pancake syrup
1½   cups half-and-half
½   teaspoon vanilla extract

Combine egg yolks and syrup in top of a double boiler, stirring well with a wire whisk. Gradually stir in half-and-half. Bring water to a boil. Reduce heat to low; cook, stirring constantly, until mixture thickens and coats back of a spoon. Remove from heat, and stir in vanilla. Serve warm or chilled. **Yield:** 2 cups.

Eggnog Custard
With Candied
Cherries

EGGNOG CUSTARDS
WITH CANDIED CHERRIES

These silky, smooth custards are as rich as they are elegant.
You'll enjoy their contrast in texture with the candy-coated
maraschino cherries that adorn them. The cherries are great
alone, too!

5   egg yolks
¼   cup plus 2 tablespoons sugar
1   teaspoon vanilla extract
¼   teaspoon salt
2   cups half-and-half
¼   cup bourbon
Ground nutmeg
Candied Cherries

Place six (6-ounce) custard cups or soufflé dishes in a 13"
x 9" x 2" baking pan; set aside. Beat first 4 ingredients
with a wire whisk until thick and pale; set aside.

Bring half-and-half to a simmer in a small heavy
saucepan; remove from heat. Gradually stir about one-
fourth of half-and-half into yolk mixture; add to remaining half-and-half, stirring constantly with a wire whisk.
Stir in bourbon.

Spoon custard mixture evenly into custard cups. Add
water to baking pan to a depth of 1". Bake, uncovered, at
325° for 45 minutes or until a knife inserted in center
comes out clean. Remove custards from water. Cool completely on a wire rack. Cover and chill 8 hours.

To serve, sprinkle custards with nutmeg, and top each
custard with 3 Candied Cherries. **Yield:** 6 servings.

CANDIED CHERRIES
18 maraschino cherries with stems
Vegetable cooking spray
½ cup sugar
¼ cup light corn syrup
2 tablespoons water

Drain cherries; place on paper towels to drain for 8 hours. Line a baking sheet with aluminum foil; coat foil with cooking spray, and set aside.

Combine sugar, corn syrup, and water in a small heavy saucepan. Place over low heat, stirring until sugar dissolves. Bring to a boil over medium heat; cover and cook 2 to 3 minutes to wash down sugar crystals from sides of pan. Uncover and cook, without stirring, until a candy thermometer registers 325° (6 to 8 minutes).

Working quickly and holding cherry by the stem, dip each cherry into hot syrup to coat. Place cherries, stem up, on foil-lined baking sheet. Let cherries cool and harden. **Yield:** 1½ dozen.

Centerpiece Desserts

Make one of these stunning Guest Star desserts, and you'll have something memorable enough to be the centerpiece for your holiday dining table. Here we show you how to make these desserts part of your tabletop decor.

Good Things Come in Small Packages: Weave individual Eggnog Custards with Candied Cherries (facing page) amongst gaily wrapped packages. If your table allows, set a custard near each guest's place.

All That Glitters Is Gold: As this book's cover photo attests, our Cheesecake Sampler (page 110) is practically a centerpiece unto itself. Surround it with sparkling gold and white ornaments, shiny ribbon, and starry Christmas garland, and your guests may ask for dessert to be the first course.

Replace Flowers with Fruit: Spiced Steamed Pudding with Maple Sauce (page 111) gets added appeal from its garnishes of pecans, walnuts, and seasonal fruits such as kumquats, lady apples, and cranberries. Place this pudding on your finest pedestal cake stand tied with Christmas ribbon, and you won't need a flowery centerpiece.

From Rustic to Rich: Versatility is the signature of the Bûche de Noël (page 109), also known as a yule log. It is inspired by the log burned on Christmas Eve and represents the triumph of light over darkness. Its showstopper appearance qualifies it to accompany both rustic family fare and a seven-course meal that pulls out all the stops. Our version of this traditional French dessert uses pistachios for "moss," scored chocolate frosting resembling bark, and mushrooms made of meringue and chocolate to liken it to a real log. Add a few bay leaves and crab apples, and you'll have a finale that will keep the conversation flowing at dinnertime.

BLUE-RIBBON ENTRÉES

This colorful variety of top-rated main dishes can take you beyond basic turkey fare this season.

Peppered Beef
Tenderloin

PEPPERED BEEF TENDERLOIN

For hotter flavor, substitute the more common black peppercorns for the less pungent green and red peppercorns.

1   (8-ounce) carton sour cream
3   tablespoons Dijon mustard
2   tablespoons prepared horseradish
2   tablespoons whole green peppercorns
2   tablespoons whole red peppercorns
2   teaspoons coarse salt
1   (3½- to 4-pound) beef tenderloin, trimmed
1   cup chopped fresh flat-leaf parsley
¼   cup butter, softened
3   tablespoons Dijon mustard
Garnishes: baby artichokes, fresh rosemary sprigs

Make-Ahead: Combine first 3 ingredients. Cover; chill.
   Place peppercorns in container of an electric blender; cover and pulse until chopped. Transfer to a bowl, and stir in salt.
   Place beef on a lightly greased rack in a shallow roasting pan. Combine parsley, butter, and 3 tablespoons mustard; rub mixture evenly over tenderloin. Pat peppercorn mixture evenly over beef. Cover; chill up to 24 hours.

When Ready to Serve: Bake at 350° for 50 minutes or until meat thermometer inserted in thickest portion of beef registers 145° (medium-rare) to 160° (medium). Transfer beef to a platter; cover loosely with aluminum foil. Let stand 10 minutes before slicing. Serve with sour cream mixture. Garnish, if desired. **Yield:** 8 servings.

TAWNY BAKED HAM

As it bakes, this succulent ham will whet eager appetites with a smoky, sweet aroma.

1   (19-pound) smoked, fully cooked whole ham*
⅓   cup Dijon mustard
1   cup firmly packed brown sugar
35   whole cloves (2 teaspoons)
2   cups apple cider
2   cups pitted whole dates
2   cups dried figs, stems removed
2   cups pitted prunes
2   cups tawny port wine
Garnishes: kumquats, blood orange halves, dried figs,
         pineapple sage leaves

Tawny Baked Ham

Remove and discard skin from ham. Make ⅛"-deep cuts in fat on ham in a diamond design. Brush mustard over top and sides of ham. Coat ham with brown sugar, pressing into mustard, if necessary.
   Using an ice pick, make a hole in center of each diamond. Insert a clove into each hole. Place ham, fat side up, in a lightly greased large shallow roasting pan. Insert meat thermometer, making sure it does not touch fat or bone. Pour apple cider into pan. Bake, uncovered, at 350° for 2 hours, basting often with apple cider.
   Combine dates and next 3 ingredients; pour into pan with ham. Bake 30 minutes or until meat thermometer registers 140°, basting often with mixture in pan; cover ham with aluminum foil to prevent burning.
   Transfer ham to a serving platter; let stand 10 minutes before slicing. Remove fruit from pan, using a slotted spoon, and set aside.
   Pour pan drippings into a large saucepan, and cook over medium-high heat until reduced by half. Stir in reserved fruit. Serve sauce with ham. Garnish, if desired. **Yield:** 35 servings.

*To save time, buy a cooked trimmed ham. All you'll need to do is score the thin layer of fat around the ham.

CROWN ROAST OF PORK WITH CHESTNUT STUFFING

1   (16-rib) crown roast of pork (about 8 pounds)
1   tablespoon vegetable oil
1   teaspoon salt
¼   teaspoon pepper
1   pound ground pork sausage
1   small onion, chopped (about ⅔ cup)
⅓   cup chopped celery
1   clove garlic, minced
8   ounces French bread, cut into ½" cubes (5½ cups)
1   (11-ounce) jar shelled chestnuts, coarsely chopped*
3   tablespoons chopped fresh parsley
1   teaspoon poultry seasoning
½   teaspoon dried thyme
⅛   teaspoon pepper
Dash of salt
½   cup half-and-half
Garnishes: lady apples, fresh thyme sprigs, flat-leaf parsley

Brush roast with oil; sprinkle on all sides with 1 teaspoon salt and ¼ teaspoon pepper. Place roast, bone ends up, in a shallow roasting pan. Insert meat thermometer, making sure it does not touch fat or bone. Bake at 475° for 15 minutes; reduce oven temperature to 325°, and bake 1 hour and 15 minutes.

Meanwhile, brown sausage in a large nonstick skillet, stirring until it crumbles. Remove from skillet, reserving 1 tablespoon drippings in skillet; drain. Cook onion, celery, and garlic in skillet over medium-high heat, stirring constantly, until tender; remove from heat.

Combine sausage, onion mixture, bread cubes, and next 6 ingredients, mixing well. Pour half-and-half over stuffing, stirring gently until blended. Spoon 3 cups stuffing into center of roast, mounding slightly. Cover stuffing and exposed ends of ribs with aluminum foil; spoon remaining stuffing into a greased 11" x 7" x 1½" baking dish.

Bake roast and dish of stuffing at 325° for 40 minutes or until thermometer registers 160°. Transfer roast to a large serving platter; remove foil. Let stand 10 minutes before carving. Garnish, if desired. **Yield:** 8 servings.

To roast your own chestnuts, you'll need 1 pound fresh chestnuts. Cut a slit in each chestnut shell. Place on an ungreased baking sheet. Bake at 400° for 15 minutes; cool. Discard shells.

Crown Roast of
Pork with Chestnut
Stuffing

Roast Duck
With Cherry Sauce

ROAST DUCK WITH CHERRY SAUCE

1   (5- to 6- pound) dressed duckling
1   small orange, quartered
2   sprigs fresh parsley
1   small onion, quartered
1   carrot, scraped and quartered
1   stalk celery, halved
½   teaspoon salt
¼   teaspoon freshly ground pepper
Garnishes: fresh cherries, fresh flat-leaf parsley sprigs,
        orange slices
Cherry Sauce

Remove giblets and neck from duckling; reserve for
another use. Rinse duckling thoroughly with cold water;
pat dry with paper towels.

Rub 1 orange quarter over skin and inside cavity of
duckling. Place remaining orange quarters, 2 parsley sprigs,
and next 3 ingredients in cavity of duckling; close cavity
with skewers. Tie ends of legs together with string. Lift
wingtips up and over back, and tuck under duckling.

Sprinkle with salt and pepper. Place duckling on a
rack in a shallow roasting pan breast side up. Insert meat

thermometer into meaty portion of thigh, making sure it
does not touch bone.

Bake, uncovered, at 425° for 45 minutes. Reduce oven
temperature to 400°; bake 35 minutes or until meat thermometer registers 180°. Turn duckling often during baking for more even browning and crisping of skin, if
desired. Transfer duckling to a serving platter; let stand 10
minutes before carving. Garnish, if desired. Serve with
Cherry Sauce. **Yield:** 4 servings.

CHERRY SAUCE

1   (16½-ounce) can Bing cherries in heavy syrup,
        undrained
½   cup sugar
1½   tablespoons cornstarch
¼   teaspoon salt
2   tablespoons red wine vinegar
2   tablespoons lemon juice

Drain cherries, reserving ⅔ cup syrup; set aside. Combine
sugar, cornstarch, and salt in a small saucepan; gradually
stir in reserved syrup. Cook over medium-high heat, stirring constantly, until thick and bubbly. Stir in cherries,
vinegar, and lemon juice; cook until heated. **Yield:** 2 cups.

LEMON-SAGE TURKEY

1 (12-pound) turkey
2 tablespoons butter or margarine, softened
2 tablespoons fresh lemon juice
8 to 10 fresh sage leaves
1 lemon, halved
1 teaspoon salt, divided
½ teaspoon freshly ground pepper, divided
Lemon-Parmesan Stuffing
2 cups dry white wine
3 tablespoons all-purpose flour
Garnishes: fresh sage leaves, lemon slices,
        lemon rind curls

Remove giblets and neck from turkey. Reserve giblets for Lemon-Parmesan Stuffing. Reserve neck for another use. Rinse turkey thoroughly with cold water; pat dry.

Combine butter and lemon juice; stir well with a wire whisk. Carefully loosen skin from turkey at neck area, working down to breast and thigh area. Rub two-thirds of lemon butter mixture under skin. Place 8 to 10 sage leaves between skin and meat. Rub inside of body and neck cavities with lemon halves. Sprinkle cavities evenly with ½ teaspoon salt and ¼ teaspoon pepper.

Lightly stuff Lemon-Parmesan Stuffing into body and neck cavities of turkey. Place turkey on a lightly greased rack in a roasting pan, breast side up. Tie legs together with heavy string. Lift wingtips up and over back, and tuck under bird.

Coat turkey with remaining one-third lemon butter mixture; sprinkle with remaining ½ teaspoon salt and ¼ teaspoon pepper. Pour wine into pan. Insert a meat thermometer into meaty portion of thigh, making sure it does not touch bone.

Bake, uncovered, at 325° for 3½ hours on bottom oven rack or until thermometer inserted into thickest part of leg registers 180° and center of stuffing reaches 165°. Let turkey stand 15 minutes before carving.

While turkey stands, pour pan drippings through a wire-mesh strainer into a large saucepan, discarding solids. Combine flour and ¾ cup pan drippings, stirring until mixture is smooth; add to remaining pan drippings in saucepan, adding enough water to measure 2¼ cups, if necessary. Bring mixture to a boil, stirring constantly; reduce heat, and simmer, uncovered, 5 minutes or until mixture is thickened, stirring often. Serve with turkey. Garnish, if desired. **Yield:** 12 servings.

Lemon-Sage
Turkey

LEMON-PARMESAN STUFFING

2 medium onions, coarsely chopped (about 2 cups)
¼ cup butter or margarine, melted
Turkey giblets, chopped
1½ cups dry white wine
2 lemons, peeled, seeded, and diced
6 cups day-old bread cubes (about 8 slices bread)
⅔ cup freshly grated Parmesan cheese
¼ cup chopped fresh parsley
2 tablespoons chopped fresh sage
1 teaspoon salt
1 teaspoon freshly ground pepper

Cook onion in butter in a large skillet over medium-high heat, stirring constantly, until tender. Add giblets and wine. Bring to a boil; cover, reduce heat, and simmer 45 minutes or until giblets are tender.

Add lemon, and cook, uncovered, 2 minutes. Place bread cubes in a large bowl.

Pour giblet mixture over bread cubes; add Parmesan cheese and remaining ingredients, tossing mixture well. **Yield:** 5 cups.

Lemon Curls: Cut long strips of rind from a lemon, using a citrus stripper or channel knife. Curl the strips around your finger or a wooden spoon handle, and remove.

TAKING SIDES

It makes perfect sense to plan simple side dishes that leave you more time for creating a spectacular entrée or dessert—or for just spending time with guests. These flexible recipes will fit effortlessly into your schedule.

French Green Beans
With Orange-Shallot Butter

FRENCH GREEN BEANS WITH ORANGE-SHALLOT BUTTER

¼ cup minced shallot
2 teaspoons grated orange rind
1 tablespoon sherry (optional)
2 tablespoons unsalted butter, softened
¼ teaspoon salt
¼ teaspoon freshly ground pepper
1 (16-ounce) package frozen French-style green beans

Place a small nonstick skillet over medium heat until hot. Add shallot; cook until tender, stirring often. Stir in orange rind and, if desired, sherry; remove from heat. Spread mixture in a single layer to cool. Combine shallot mixture, butter, salt, and pepper; cover and chill.

Cook green beans according to package directions; drain. Place beans in a serving dish; spoon butter mixture over beans. Toss beans gently before serving. **Yield:** 6 servings.

WILTED WINTER GREENS

3 pounds fresh turnip greens*
1 cup water
3 tablespoons extra virgin olive oil
3 cloves garlic, pressed
¾ teaspoon dried crushed red pepper
¼ teaspoon salt
2 teaspoons fresh lemon juice

Remove stems from greens. Wash leaves thoroughly in cold water; drain. Repeat procedure. Tear leaves into bite-size pieces.

Bring water to a boil in a Dutch oven; gradually add turnip greens, stirring until greens begin to wilt. Cover and cook over medium heat 10 minutes or until greens are tender; drain well, and set greens aside.

Heat oil in Dutch oven; add garlic and pepper. Cook, stirring constantly, 2 minutes or just until garlic begins to brown. Add greens, and toss well. Cook until thoroughly heated, stirring occasionally. Sprinkle with salt and lemon juice; toss gently. **Yield:** 4 servings.

You can substitute 1 (2-pound) package fresh torn turnip greens for loose greens, if desired; remove any large stems, and tear large leaves into bite-size pieces.

GLAZED BEETS WITH CLOVES AND PORT

If you're not a fan of port wine, cranberry juice substitutes nicely. Pair either up with a few ingredients you've probably got on hand, and you've got a colorful side dish for pork or beef.

2 tablespoons butter or margarine
2 tablespoons brown sugar
¾ teaspoon salt
½ teaspoon freshly ground pepper
½ teaspoon ground cloves
½ cup port wine or cranberry juice
2 (15-ounce) cans sliced beets, drained

Melt butter in a large skillet over medium-low heat. Stir in brown sugar and next 3 ingredients; cook until sugar melts. Stir in port; cook over medium-high heat until mixture is slightly thickened. Add beets to skillet; toss to coat. Cook 5 minutes or until beets are thoroughly heated. **Yield:** 6 servings.

PASTA WITH CREAMY ALFREDO SAUCE

Commercial Alfredo sauce is the secret to getting this dish on the table quickly. And if it's just the two of you, consider serving it with a salad and bread for a fast one-dish meal.

1 tablespoon olive oil
⅓ cup diced cooked ham
1 large sweet red pepper, diced
1 clove garlic, minced
1 (10-ounce) container fresh Alfredo sauce (we tested with Contadina)
1 tablespoon chopped fresh sage
½ teaspoon freshly ground pepper
2 cups bow-tie pasta, uncooked
¼ cup freshly grated Parmesan cheese

Heat oil in a large skillet over medium-high heat. Add ham, red pepper, and garlic; cook 3 minutes, stirring often. Reduce heat to medium-low; stir in Alfredo sauce, sage, and pepper. Cook, stirring constantly, until thoroughly heated.

Meanwhile, cook pasta according to package directions; drain. Add pasta to skillet; toss well. Sprinkle with cheese. **Yield:** 4 side-dish or 2 main-dish servings.

Black-Eyed Peas with Caramelized Onions And Country Ham

BLACK-EYED PEAS WITH CARAMELIZED ONION AND COUNTRY HAM

3   (15.8-ounce) cans packed from fresh shelled
    black-eyed peas (we tested with Bush's Best)
1   bay leaf
1   (14½-ounce) can ready-to-serve chicken broth
2   tablespoons olive oil
1   large purple onion, diced
¼   pound country ham, diced
½   cup balsamic vinegar
1½ teaspoons chopped fresh thyme or ½ teaspoon dried
    thyme
½   teaspoon freshly ground pepper
Garnish: fresh thyme sprigs

Combine first 3 ingredients in a 2-quart saucepan; bring to a boil. Cover, reduce heat, and simmer 10 minutes; drain. Discard bay leaf. Return peas to pan; cover and set aside.

Meanwhile, heat oil in a large skillet over medium-high heat. Add onion; cook 5 minutes or until golden, stirring often. Reduce heat; add ham, and cook 10 additional minutes or until ham is crisp and onion is well browned. Stir in vinegar, chopped thyme, and pepper; bring to a boil. Cook, stirring occasionally to loosen any caramelized bits from bottom of pan, 5 minutes or until mixture is a thin syrup. Pour over peas; toss well. Garnish, if desired. **Yield:** 8 servings.

EASY PEACH DISH

3   (15-ounce) cans peach halves in heavy syrup, drained
¼   cup firmly packed brown sugar
1   teaspoon ground cinnamon
Dash of ground nutmeg
3   tablespoons butter or margarine, cut up

Place peach halves in an 11" x 7" x 1½" baking dish. Sprinkle with brown sugar, cinnamon, and nutmeg; dot with butter. Bake, uncovered, at 325° for 45 minutes. **Yield:** 6 servings.

GINGERED PEARS IN ACORN SQUASH

3   medium acorn squash
2   ripe red pears, chopped (about 3 cups)
½   cup firmly packed brown sugar
2   teaspoons minced fresh ginger
⅓   cup butter or margarine, melted
½   teaspoon hazelnut-flavored liqueur (optional)
½   cup chopped toasted hazelnuts*

Make a small cut into each squash; microwave at HIGH 1 to 2 minutes to ease halving squash. Cut squash in half crosswise; remove and discard seeds. Place squash, cut side up, in a 13" x 9" x 2" baking dish.

Combine pear, brown sugar, ginger, butter, and, if desired, liqueur; spoon evenly into squash halves. Add boiling water to a depth of ½" to dish. Cover and bake at 350° for 1 hour and 15 minutes or until squash is tender. Transfer squash to a serving dish; sprinkle with toasted hazelnuts. **Yield:** 6 servings.

*To remove hazelnut skins, cook hazelnuts with 1 teaspoon baking soda in boiling water 30 to 45 seconds. Drain nuts; rub with dish towel (skins come right off). Dry before toasting.

Gingered Pears in Acorn Squash

GIFTS OF THE SEASON

You make it special when you make it by hand. These gift ideas are short on execution and long on thoughtfulness.

MAKE IT PERSONAL

The people on your list will feel honored when they receive gifts that have been personalized with their name or initials.

MONOGRAMMED VASE ▲
Clean and dry the vase thoroughly. Center and affix a self-adhesive vinyl letter to the front of the vase. Use masking tape to evenly frame the letter. Press the letter and tape securely to the vase, smoothing out any wrinkles. Following manufacturer's instructions, apply etching cream to the vase. Wait five minutes before washing the cream off. Dry the vase completely. Remove the tape and the letter. For materials, see Sources, page 154.

PERSONALIZED ORNAMENTS ▶
Transform plain, inexpensive ornaments into treasured mementos. Use a paint pen to write initials or names. Add dots and swirls for an overall decoration.

For a pretty presentation, tie a bow through the hanging loop at the top of each ornament. These are good gifts for teachers and neighbors, and they're quick to make.

INITIAL WREATH ▲

Using the alphabet on page 152, trace the letter of your choice onto a piece of paper. On a photocopier, enlarge the letter to the desired size. Cut out the letter to use as a pattern.

Using the pattern, trace the letter onto a sheet of Styrofoam. Cut out the letter from Styrofoam using a sharp knife. Cover the Styrofoam shape with sheet moss, using U-shaped floral pins (or floral wire cut into 2" pieces and bent to form a U) to hold the moss in place; or hot-glue the moss onto the shape, if desired. Pin or glue a length of ribbon to the back of the wreath for a hanger. Embellish the wreath with ribbon as desired, pinning or gluing to hold it in place.

MONOGRAMMED NAPKINS

Wash, dry, and iron plain, purchased napkins. Don't use fabric softener. Using a color copier (or a local quick copy center), copy the alphabet on page 147 onto iron-on transfer paper. For iron-on transfer paper, see Sources, page 154.

Cut out the desired letter from the transfer sheet, leaving as much excess paper around the letter as possible. Place a piece of paper under the napkin to prevent the design from bleeding through. Place the transfer facedown in the center of the right side of the napkin. Pin it in place. Place a hot iron (no steam) on top of the transfer. Hold the iron in place for 5 to 10 seconds. Do not slide the iron or it may smear the design. Carefully peel the transfer paper away from the napkin. You will need to use a new transfer sheet initial for each napkin.

INITIAL WRAPS

Create your own gift wrap designs by stamping kraft paper with an initial stamp—either your own initial or the gift recipient's. Either way, it's a unique way to embellish plain paper. We colored the design with a felt tip pen.

129

WINNING RIBBONS

Ribbons can do more than tie a bow. Take inspiration from these fresh ideas for gifts and decorations.

RIBBON ORNAMENTS

To make the ribbon tree and wreath ornaments, machine-baste a line of stitches down the center of a 45" length of ribbon. Tie the thread ends at one end. Cut a piece of 22-gauge wire the same length as the ribbon. Run the end of the wire under the tied end of the stitching; loop the wire to secure it to the ribbon. Using a wide zigzag stitch, stitch over the basting thread and the wire.

Using the basting thread, gather the ribbon to a length of 10"-12". Knot the basting thread ends to secure. Trim the wire and loop it to secure it to the thread. Evenly distribute the gathers.

To shape the tree, bend the wire in an S shape, gradually increasing the width to obtain the desired tree shape. Sew on small charms, if desired. Hot-glue a small piece of trim to the bottom of the tree for the trunk.

To shape the wreath, connect the ends of the wire to form a circle. Hot-glue a bow to the wreath, if desired. Thread a piece of wire or cording through the top of the wreath to form a hanger.

RIBBON TREE

To make the ribbon tree, spray-paint a Styrofoam tree form gold. Wrap the tree with wide (6") gold mesh ribbon or tulle, securing it with straight pins.

Cut lengths of 1½"- to 2½"-wide gold, copper, and silver sheer ribbons long enough to extend from underneath the tree up one side, over the top, and back down the other side to the bottom, allowing enough extra length to gather the ribbon slightly. Run a gathering stitch along the center of each length of ribbon. Gather the ribbon lengths slightly. (The 12" tree shown here uses 16 lengths of ribbon.)

Using straight pins, pin the gathered ribbon lengths on the topiary. Begin pinning underneath the tree, taking the ribbon up one side, over the top, and back down the other side, pinning the other end of the ribbon underneath the tree. Continue until the entire tree is covered.

For a tree garland, tie a small string of plastic pearls at intervals to a narrow metallic ribbon. Wind the garland around the tree, gluing it at intervals to hold it in place. If desired, wrap the trunk of the tree with silver cording, using glue to hold the cording in place. For the tree topper, we used a Christmas ornament turned upside down and pressed into the point of the tree.

RIBBON WREATH

To make the wreath, tie 2½" lengths of wired ribbon around a Styrofoam wreath form, tying the ribbons into fluffy bows. Trim the ribbon ends into an inverted V shape. The wreath pictured uses 36 lengths of ribbon on a 10" wreath form.

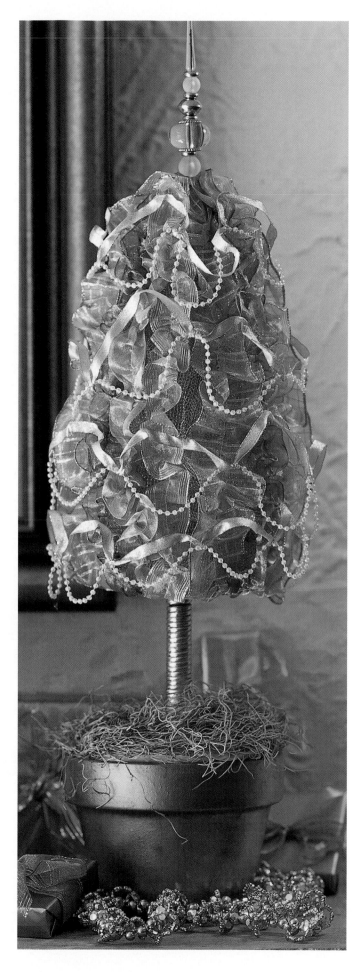

KITCHEN TOPIARIES

*Spread a little Christmas cheer to a friend's kitchen
with a gift that's both decorative and practical.*

NUTTY TOPIARIES

*Glue boxwood greenery around pots and fill with nuts for clever
holiday snack bowls.*

To add greenery to the pots, form small bunches of 2-3
boxwood pieces, wrapping the stems with green floral tape.
The number of bunches you need will depend on the
diameter of the pot. Using floral wire, wire the bunches
together lengthwise to make a garland, overlapping the
boxwood bunches to cover the taped stems. Wire the ends
of the garland, forming a wreath to fit snugly around the
top rim of the pot. Hot-glue the wreath to the pot.

For easy gift-giving, wrap the nut-filled pot with clear
cellophane and tie with a ribbon bow.

GARLIC GLOBES

This gift can last indefinitely. After the garlic is used, the topiary can be studded with other trimmings, such as dried flowers, dried citrus slices, or fancy ribbons.

To make the garlic globe, use hot glue or floral tape to secure a double-globe topiary form with base into the container of your choice. Using U-shaped floral pins (or floral wire cut into 2" pieces and bent to form a U), pin sheet moss to the top of the pot so the bottom of the topiary form does not show. Cover the topiary form with moss, using floral pins to secure it.

Using wire cutters, cut floral picks into 2" pieces, cutting at a slant to give the picks a point. Push a pick halfway into the bottom of each garlic head and push the opposite end of the pick into the topiary form to hold the garlic in place.

BAY LEAF TREE

This is a welcome treat for an herb enthusiast.

To make the bay leaf tree, use hot glue or floral tape to secure a tree-shaped topiary form with base into the container of your choice. Using U-shaped floral pins (or floral wire cut into 2" pieces and bent to form a U), pin sheet moss to the top of the pot so the bottom of the topiary form does not show.

Starting at the bottom of the tree, attach bay leaves in rows around the topiary using straight pins to hold the leaves in place and hiding the pins from the previous row with the next row of leaves. Continue until you reach the top of the tree. Top each tree with a Bouquet Garni herb sachet (recipe below).

BOUQUET GARNI

Combine bay leaves, garlic cloves, and equal amounts of dried onion flakes, peppercorns, dried whole thyme, dried parsley flakes, and dried whole marjoram in a small bowl; toss gently. Place 2 teaspoons of the herb mixture in the center of a 5" square of cheesecloth. Tie with a string and attach a note that describes the uses of bouquets garnis in seasoning soups, stews, and stocks.

Garlic
Globes

Bay
Leaf
Tree

Bouquet
Garni

No-Cook Food Gifts

These edible gifts keep your kitchen time to a minimum.
You "mix" the recipe but leave the cooking to someone else.

QUICK FRUITED SALSA

2   (11-ounce) cans mandarin oranges, drained
1   (8-ounce) can pineapple tidbits in juice, drained
1   (15-ounce) can black beans, rinsed and drained
1   sweet red pepper, chopped
½   cup chopped purple onion
1   tablespoon dried cilantro
2   tablespoons chopped canned jalapeño
1   tablespoon lime juice
¼   teaspoon minced garlic

Drain oranges; let stand on several layers of paper towels to absorb excess moisture. Snip orange slices in half using kitchen shears.

Combine pineapple and remaining 7 ingredients in a medium bowl, mixing well. Add oranges, stirring gently to combine. Spoon mixture into wide-mouth jars; seal and refrigerate. Serve as an appetizer with tortilla chips or as an accompaniment to chicken, fish, or pork.
Yield: 5 cups.

WINTER FRUIT CRISP

We give you two filling options for this dessert. If you'd like to include the fillings in your gift basket to make both variations, be sure to double the ingredients for the Oatmeal-Walnut Crumble Topping. And don't forget to include the recipe below for baking.

1   recipe Mixed Berry Filling or Golden Apple Filling
¼   cup butter
2   cups Oatmeal-Walnut Crumble Topping

Spoon fruit filling into a greased 9" square pan. Cut butter into Oatmeal-Walnut Crumble Topping until mixture is crumbly. Sprinkle topping evenly over filling. Bake at 350° for 35 minutes or until golden and bubbly. Serve warm with vanilla ice cream. **Yield:** 6 servings.

MIXED BERRY FILLING

½   cup sugar
¼   cup plus 2 tablespoons all-purpose flour
2   (12-ounce) containers cranberry-raspberry crushed
       fruit (we used Ocean Spray)
2   cups frozen blueberries

Combine sugar and flour in a medium bowl, stirring well. Add remaining ingredients, mixing well. **Yield:** 4 cups.

GOLDEN APPLE FILLING

1   cup diced dried apricots
1   cup diced dates
1   cup boiling water
3   tablespoons firmly packed brown sugar
3   tablespoons all-purpose flour
1   (20-ounce) can sliced apples, drained

Combine first 3 ingredients in a 2-cup glass measure; let stand at room temperature 1 hour.

   Combine sugar and flour in a medium bowl, stirring well. Add fruit mixture and apples to flour mixture, stirring until blended. **Yield:** 4 cups.

OATMEAL-WALNUT CRUMBLE TOPPING

1   cup regular oats, uncooked
¼   cup firmly packed brown sugar
3   tablespoons all-purpose flour
¼   teaspoon ground cinnamon
Dash of salt
½   cup chopped walnuts

Combine all ingredients in a medium bowl, stirring well. **Yield:** 2 cups.

EASY CHEESECAKE SAMPLER

Impress your friends and give our Cheesecake Sampler (page 110) as a No-Cook Food Gift. Just start with a frozen commercial cheesecake instead of our homemade cheesecake. You can top one cheesecake with all 8 toppings or buy 8 cheesecakes, top each with a different topping, and then mix and match to make 8 different gifts. We found that hatboxes are just the right size for wrapping. Refrigerate until ready to give.

GOOD MORNING PANCAKES

You can give all the pancake toppings or just one in your gift basket. Attach a card with the following cooking directions for the pancake mix: To make pancakes, add 1 large egg, 1 cup buttermilk, and 1 tablespoon vegetable oil to pancake mix. Beat, using a wire whisk, until blended.

HEARTY CORNMEAL PANCAKE MIX

1   cup all-purpose flour
3   tablespoons yellow cornmeal
2   tablespoons brown sugar
1   tablespoon baking powder
½   teaspoon baking soda
½   teaspoon salt

Combine all ingredients in a medium bowl, stirring until blended. Spoon mix into a heavy-duty, zip-top plastic bag; remove air, and seal. **Yield:** 1½ cups.

PRALINE CRUNCH SYRUP

1½ cups maple-flavored syrup
½   cup chopped toasted pecans (toasting optional)
2   (1.4-ounce) English toffee candy bars, crushed

Combine all ingredients in a small bowl, stirring gently until blended. Using a wide-mouthed funnel, transfer to a bottle; seal. **Yield:** 2½ cups.

LEMON-BERRY SYRUP

1   cup strawberry jam
½   cup frozen lemonade concentrate, thawed and undiluted
1   cup frozen blueberries

Combine all ingredients in a small bowl, stirring gently until blended. Using a wide-mouthed funnel, transfer syrup to a bottle; seal. **Yield:** 2½ cups.

GEORGIA PEACH HONEY

1   cup honey
¾   cup peach jam
¼   cup orange juice

Combine all ingredients in a medium bowl, stirring until blended. Using a wide-mouthed funnel, transfer to a bottle; seal. **Yield:** 2 cups.

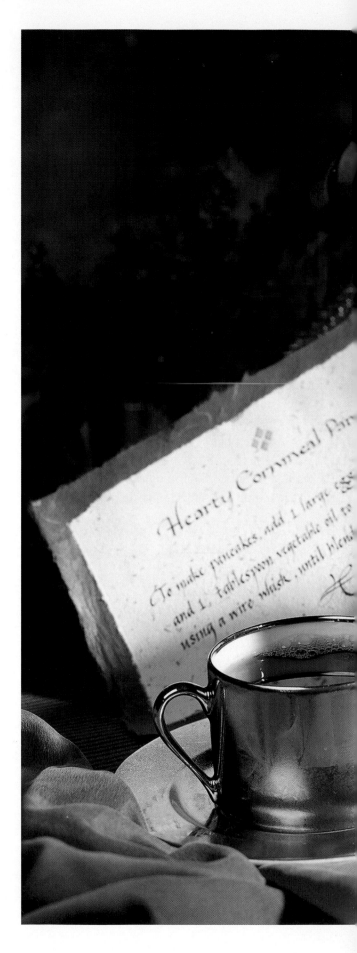

ASSEMBLED AND DELIVERED

Personal yet practical, gift baskets are a tried-and-true solution in the quest for the perfect present. Here are some ingenious ideas for packaging—and, once the contents are gone, the container can be put to other good uses.

Stationery
Stash

A vintage tin lunch box filled with fun writing supplies will inspire the letter-writer on your list.

Coffee to Go

Offer a friend a coffee break—gourmet blends and handy utensils wrapped up in a snazzy wire basket.

Little Luxuries

Give someone special carte blanche to indulge with a large acrylic bowl filled with soaps, bubble bath gels, candles, and fluffy slippers.

Cookie Kit

Inspire a fledgling baker or a well-seasoned pro with tools of the trade, including cookie cutters and colorful sprinkles, all stacked in a pretty pie tin.

Shoeshine Box

A bright smile is what you'll get when you give this shoe kit all suited up in a tool box.

WRAPPED IN STYLE

*It's all in the presentation, and these ideas will
make your gifts almost too pretty to open.*

◀ CANNED GOODS

Wash and dry an empty potato chip can. Cut a piece of fabric large enough to wrap the entire can, allowing enough fabric to fold over the top of the can. Turn under the raw edge of the fabric at the seam, and glue the fabric in place along the seam and on the inside of the can at the top. Glue ribbon or fabric trim along the bottom of the can to hide the raw edge of the fabric.

For the top, spray-paint the plastic top gold. Let dry. Punch a hole in the center of the top and thread cording or tassels through the hole, knotting the cording on the back side of the lid to hold it in place. This makes an excellent container for candles or cookies.

BAUBLES AND BOWS ▼

Tie a large, ornate bead into the bow of a wide ribbon for a quick but fancy gift wrap. Old chandelier pendants found at flea markets or tag sales are just right for this packaging idea.

SWEET TREATS

Use two colors of ribbon and a handful of candy canes to tie up a tasty-looking package.

TREE TOPPER

Glue peppermints in the shape of a tree onto a wrapped package. Glue on cinnamon sticks for the trunk. Wrap wired ribbon around the package at the base of the tree, and glue on a clipping of tinsel at the top.

AU NATUREL

A bow is unnecessary when a gift is decorated with discoveries from the garden. Brown wrapping paper provides the perfect background for a handful of natural treasures.

PETITE GIFT POUCHES

Punch holes in two squares of handmade paper, weave ribbon through the holes, fill the pouch with a tiny gift, and tie the ribbon in a bow for a beautiful little package. Stamp an initial or other design on the front, if desired.

STAR ANISE CARD

Using crisscross stitches, hand-sew the desired number of star anise onto the front of a plain gift enclosure card. Write a greeting on the card and place it in an envelope.

CHRISTMAS TIN GREETING

Cut colored paper to fit the lid of a small tin. Using jewelry glue, affix a charm or button to the center of the lid. Let dry. Write a greeting on the colored paper with a paint pen. Let dry. Glue on a bow.

ORNAMENT CARD

Write a greeting on a plain gift enclosure card. Loop a ribbon through the hanger of a delicate ornament. Punch a hole in the card and thread the ribbon through the hole. Tuck the card and ornament into an envelope.

FRAMED FOR GIVING

Insert a handwritten or stenciled greeting in a small photo frame for a gift tag that does double duty as a gift on its own.

QUICK GIFTS

Try these quick solutions for last-minute gifts and party favors that you can make by the handful.

PEPPERMINT WRAPS

Stack peppermint candy sticks evenly together. Coil copper wire around the candy, adding a decorative bead with each wrap of the wire. Continue wrapping, bending the end of the wire slightly to prevent a sharp edge. Repeat on the opposite end of the candy stick stack.

CHRISTMAS CONES ▶

Transfer the cone pattern on page 153 to tracing paper. Cut out the pattern and place it on top of sturdy gift wrapping paper. Cut out the cone. Roll the paper into a cone and glue the long edge in place. Let dry. (Use a clothespin or paper clip to hold the edges together until the glue is dry.)

Glue fabric trim such as rickrack around the top of the cone. Let dry. Glue the ends of a length of fabric trim inside the top of the cone to form a hanger. Let dry.

Fill the cone with holiday treats such as miniature toys, candy canes, or flowers.

POTPOURRI PILLOWS ▶

For one pillow: Cut an 18" length of 4¾"-wide wired ribbon. Fold the cut edges under ½". Glue the edges down. Let dry. Fold the glued ends of the ribbon toward the center, overlapping the ends approximately 2". Glue along the long sides of the ribbon. Let dry.

Fill the pillow to the desired fullness with potpourri. Tie a ribbon bow around the pillow, or create a stack of several pillows and tie them together with ribbon.

RIBBON BOOKMARKS ▶

Insert 2" of an 18" length of 1½"-wide ribbon through a 10mm jump ring (available at craft and discount stores). Fold the ribbon to the back. Using fusible web tape, iron the ribbon in place.

Place charms and beads on a 5mm jump ring. Using needlenose pliers, attach the charms to the 10mm jump ring. Cut a V-shaped notch in the end of the ribbon.

PATTERNS

MAKING A GARLAND *See page 32.*

For the garland, use a variety of evergreens for an interesting mix of textures and different shades of green. The more greenery you use, the fuller the garland will be.

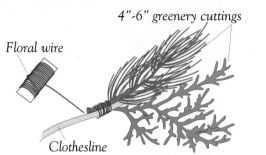

Floral wire

4"-6" greenery cuttings

Clothesline

1. Lay bundles of 2 to 3 greenery cuttings on one end of a length of clothesline that measures the desired garland length. Wrap the stems tightly with floral wire.

2. Lay second bundle of greenery over the ends of the first. Spiral the wire down the stems, wrapping tightly.

3. Continue wiring bundles to the clothesline, working all the way around the clothesline and keeping the stems pointing in the same direction. Attach the last bundle of greenery with the stems pointing in the opposite direction, hiding the stem ends among the foliage.

OVER-THE-TOP HOLIDAY STYLE
Instructions begin on page 45.

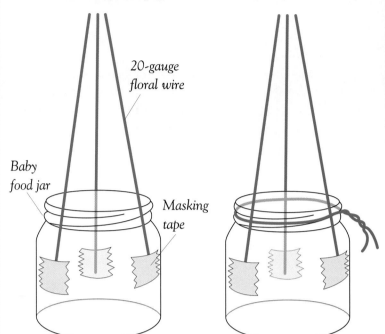

20-gauge floral wire

Baby food jar

Masking tape

1. Cut 3 lengths of floral wire and tape to jar as shown.

2. Wrap floral wire around the taped wires and twist tightly around the neck of the jar.

3. Untape the wires and bend the ends up and over the collar wire, twisting tightly. Twist the 3 wires together at the top, bending them to form a hook. Tie a ribbon around the jar and put a tea light inside.

MONOGRAMMED NAPKINS

Instructions begin on page 129.

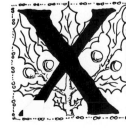  

No-Sew Noel Stocking

Instructions begin on page 60.

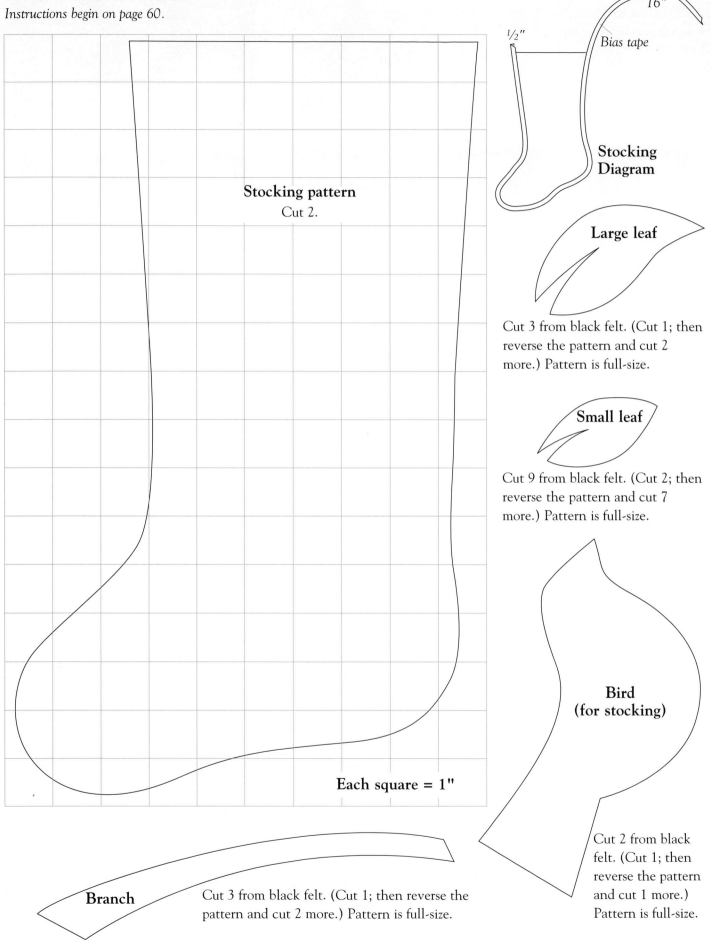

Stocking pattern
Cut 2.

Each square = 1"

Stocking Diagram

1/2"   16"   *Bias tape*

Large leaf

Cut 3 from black felt. (Cut 1; then reverse the pattern and cut 2 more.) Pattern is full-size.

Small leaf

Cut 9 from black felt. (Cut 2; then reverse the pattern and cut 7 more.) Pattern is full-size.

Bird (for stocking)

Cut 2 from black felt. (Cut 1; then reverse the pattern and cut 1 more.) Pattern is full-size.

Branch   Cut 3 from black felt. (Cut 1; then reverse the pattern and cut 2 more.) Pattern is full-size.

NO-SEW NOEL ORNAMENTS

Instructions begin on page 60.
Patterns are full-size.
Bird and wing patterns for ornaments are on page 150.

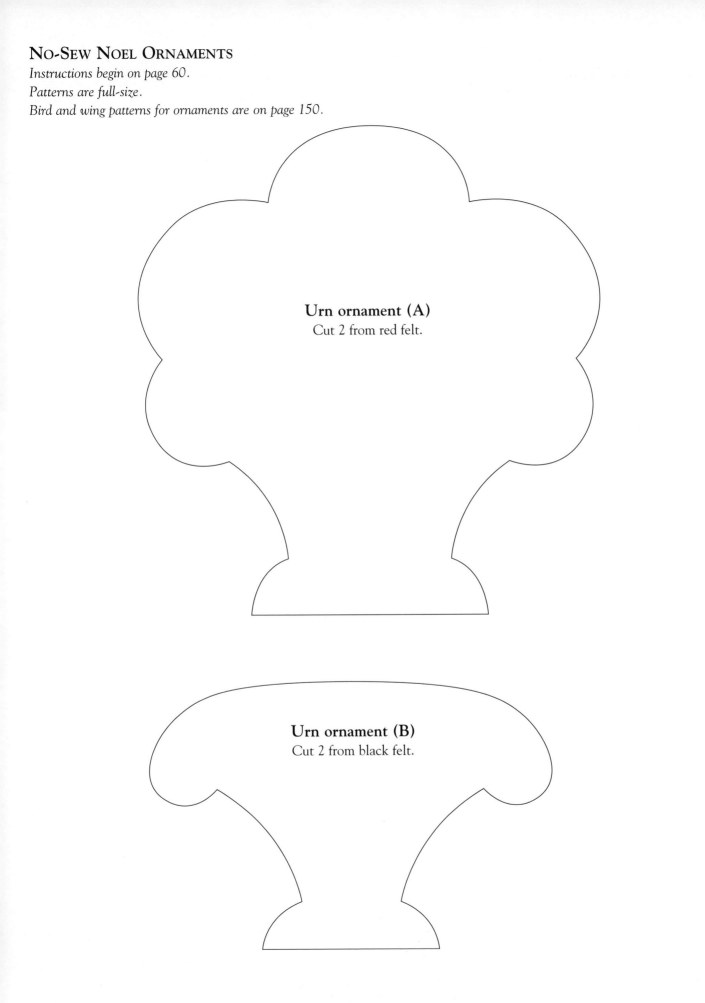

Urn ornament (A)
Cut 2 from red felt.

Urn ornament (B)
Cut 2 from black felt.

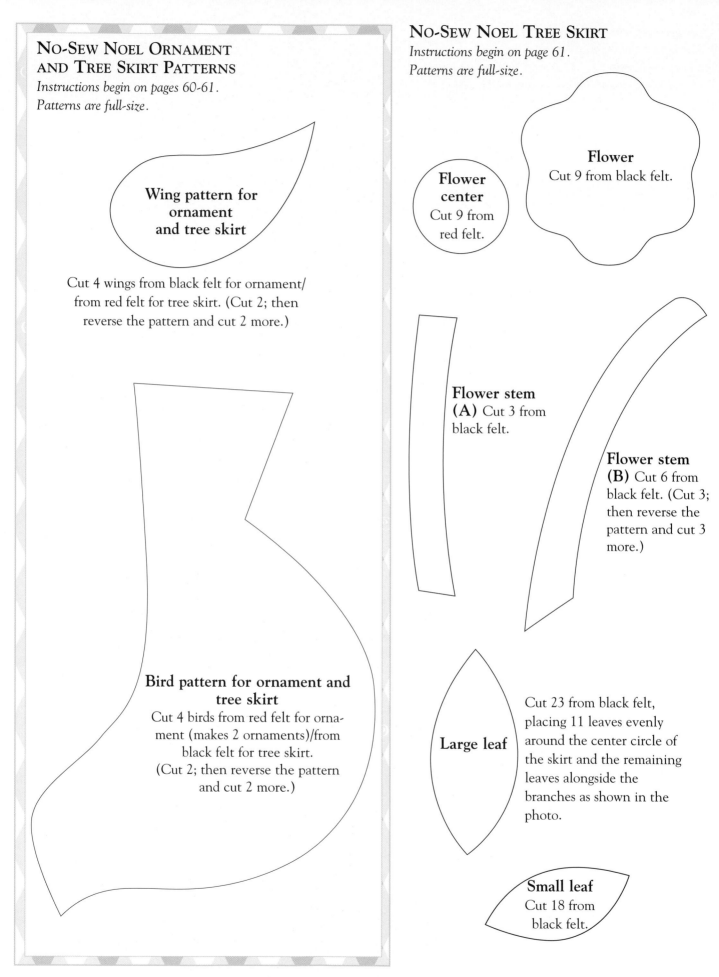

NO-SEW NOEL ORNAMENT AND TREE SKIRT PATTERNS

Instructions begin on pages 60-61.
Patterns are full-size.

Wing pattern for ornament and tree skirt

Cut 4 wings from black felt for ornament/ from red felt for tree skirt. (Cut 2; then reverse the pattern and cut 2 more.)

Bird pattern for ornament and tree skirt
Cut 4 birds from red felt for ornament (makes 2 ornaments)/from black felt for tree skirt. (Cut 2; then reverse the pattern and cut 2 more.)

NO-SEW NOEL TREE SKIRT

Instructions begin on page 61.
Patterns are full-size.

Flower center
Cut 9 from red felt.

Flower
Cut 9 from black felt.

Flower stem (A) Cut 3 from black felt.

Flower stem (B) Cut 6 from black felt. (Cut 3; then reverse the pattern and cut 3 more.)

Large leaf

Cut 23 from black felt, placing 11 leaves evenly around the center circle of the skirt and the remaining leaves alongside the branches as shown in the photo.

Small leaf
Cut 18 from black felt.

NO-SEW NOEL TREE SKIRT
Instructions begin on page 61.
Patterns are full-size.

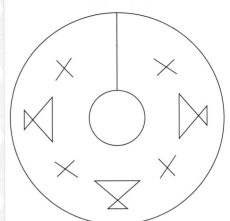

Tree Skirt Diagram

Picture the tree skirt as a clock; place the urns at 3:00, 6:00, and 9:00. Place the four birds/branches at the Xs.

Large urn
Cut 3 from black felt.

Branch
Cut 4 from black felt. (Cut 2; then reverse the pattern and cut 2 more.)

CHRISTMAS CONES

Instructions begin on page 145.
Pattern is full-size.

Cone pattern

MAKING A BOW

1. For an 8"-wide bow, you will need 4 yards of wired ribbon. To make the bow, measure 4" from the end of the ribbon. Pinch the ribbon between your forefinger and thumb. (This is the center point of the bow.) Make a 4" loop and pinch the ribbon again at the center.

2. Twist the ribbon one-half turn and make a loop on the opposite side. Make 5 loops on either side of the center in the same manner. Fold a 9" length of floral wire over the center of the bow.

3. Fold the bow in half across the wire. Twist the wire ends together. Fluff the bow by pulling firmly on the loops. To add streamers to the bow, cut ribbon into the desired lengths and secure them with wire to the back of the bow.

SOURCES

Information current at time of publication

Pages 8–9—garlands: Contact Laurel Springs Christmas Tree Farm, P.O. Box 85, Hwy. 18 S., Laurel Springs, NC 28644-0085. Call (800) 851-2345 for a free catalog.

Pages 16–17—plate: Contact Bromberg's, 2800 Cahaba Rd., Birmingham, AL 35352, or call (205) 871-3276.

Page 33—Styrofoam ball: To find a Michael's Arts and Craft Store nearest you, call (800) 642-4235.

Page 38—stockings: Contact Pottery Barn at (800) 922-5507.

Page 39—oasis wreath: Contact Galveston Wreath Company, 1124 25th Street, Galveston, TX 77550-4409, or call (409) 765-8597.

Page 40–41—candles: Contact Ana Design, 1 Ott Street, Trenton, NJ 08638, or call (203) 748-0696.

Page 42—ornaments: Contact Marguerite's Conceits, 2406 Canterbury Road, Mountain Brook, AL 35243, or call (205) 879-2730.

napkins: Contact Crate & Barrel at (800) 451-8217.

Page 45—ornaments: Contact The Company Store at (800) 285-3696.

Page 46–47—Styrofoam ball: To find a Michael's Arts and Craft Store nearest you, call (800) 642-4235.

candles: Contact Ana Design, 1 Ott Street, Trenton, NJ 08638, or call (203) 748-0696.

Page 50–51—bead garland and ornaments: Contact Smith & Hawken at (800) 776-5558.

Page 55—candles: Contact Ana Design, 1 Ott Street, Trenton, NJ 08638, or call (203) 748-0696.

Page 56–57—beads: Contact Beadbox Inc., 10135 East Via Linda, Suite C-116, Scottsdale, AZ 85258-5312.

Page 58–61—felt: Contact Kunin Felt at www.kuninfelt.com, or call (603) 929-6100 for mail-order prices.

Page 62–65—hard peppermints: Contact Hammond's Candies Since 1920, 2550 West 29th Avenue, Denver, CO 80211, or call (888) CANDY-99.

Page 78—plate: Contact Horchow, P.O. Box 620048, Dallas, TX 75262-0048, or call (800) 456-7000.

Page 82—plate: Contact Marge Margulie's Pottery, 90 E. Church Lane, Philadelphia, PA 19144, or call (214) 844-9603.

Page 84—platter: Contact Christine's, 2822 Petticoat Lane, Birmingham, AL 35223, or call (205) 871-8297.

gold and white ribbon: Contact Vaban Gille, Inc., P.O. Box 420747, San Francisco, CA 94142, or call (417) 552-5490.

velvet ribbon: Contact Ribbtrim, Inc., 561 7th Avenue, New York, NY 10018, or call (212) 221-6663.

Page 86—pitcher: Contact Bromberg's, 2800 Cahaba Rd., Birmingham, AL 35352, or call (205) 871-3276.

Page 89—plates and flatware: Contact Bromberg's, 2800 Cahaba Rd., Birmingham, AL 35352, or call (205) 871-3276.

Page 90—ribbon: Contact Vaban Gille, Inc., P.O. Box 420747, San Francisco, CA 94142, or call (417) 552-5490.

Page 94—plate: Contact Bromberg's, 2800 Cahaba Rd., Birmingham, AL 35352, or call (205) 871-3276.

sheer green ribbon: Contact Vaban Gille, Inc., P.O. Box 420747, San Francisco, CA 94142, or call (417) 552-5490.

velvet ribbon: Contact Ribbtrim, Inc., 561 7th Avenue, New York, NY 10018, or call (212) 221-6663.

Page 96—ribbon: Contact Vaban Gille, Inc., P.O. Box 420747, San Francisco, CA 94142, or call (417) 552-5490.

Page 99—mug: Contact Bell Cottage, 3816 W. Magnolia Blvd., Burbank, CA 91505, or call (818) 841-8415.

Page 101—angel Springerle mold: Contact The-House-On-the-Hill, P.O. Box 7003, Villa Park, IL 60181, or call (630) 969-2624.

Page 112—ramekins: Contact Woodbury Pewter, 860 Main Street South, Woodbury, CT 06778, or call (800) 648-2014.

ribbon: Contact Vaban Gille, Inc., P.O. Box 420747, San Francisco, CA 94142, or call (417) 552-5490.

Page 120—bowl: Contact Smith & Hawken at (800) 776-5558.

ribbon: Contact Vaban Gille, Inc., P.O. Box 420747, San Francisco, CA 94142, or call (417) 552-5490.

Page 123—plate: Contact Marge Margulie's Pottery, 90 E. Church Lane, Philadelphia, PA 19144, or call (214) 844-9603.

Page 126—etching cream: To find a Michael's Arts and Craft Store nearest you, call (800) 642-4235.

Page 129—iron-on transfer paper: Contact Hues, Inc., 936 Historic West 8th Street, Anderson, IN 46016, or call (765) 642-9308.

Page 130–131—ribbon: Contact Vaban Gille, Inc., P.O. Box 420747, San Francisco, CA 94142, or call (417) 552-5490.

Page 133—topiary form: To find a Michael's Arts and Craft Store nearest you, call (800) 642-4235.

Page 134—wire basket: To find a Pier 1 Imports nearest you, call (800) 447-4371.

ribbon: Contact Vaban Gille, Inc., P.O. Box 420747, San Francisco, CA 94142, or call (417) 552-5490.

Page 136–137—wire basket: To find a Pier 1 Imports nearest you, call (800) 447-4371.

ribbon: Contact Vaban Gille, Inc., P.O. Box 420747, San Francisco, CA 94142, or call (417) 552-5490.

cup and saucer: Contact Bromberg's, 2800 Cahaba Rd., Birmingham, AL 35352, or call (205) 871-3276.

GENERAL INDEX

Apple votive holders, 41

Bay leaf topiary, 133
beads
    candles, 57
    gift bag ties, 141
    icicle ornaments, 57
    napkin rings, 56
bookmarks, ribbon, 145
bountiful harvest tree, 34
bouquet garni, 133
bow, how-to, 153

Candles. *See also* votive holders.
    beaded, 57
    floating, 48
    gift containers for, 140
    in coarse salt, 46
    silver-trimmed, 49
    with cranberries and apples, 55
candleholders, moss and ribbon, 47
candle pots, gilt-leaf, 49
candle rings, pinecone, 46
candy dish, peppermint, 63
centerpieces, 8, 10, 26, 48, 50, 54, 55, 62
chandeliers, 44, 52
cone, gift, 145
cutting guide, greenery, 33

Door decorations, 28

Floating candles, 48
front door basket, 28
fruit
    centerpiece, 54, 55
    chandelier, 52
    decorating with, 52-55
    pomanders, 53

Garlands, 8, 32, 38
    how-to, 146
garlic globe topiary, 133
gift wraps
    bags with beads, 141
    cone, 145
    containers, 138–140
    personalized wraps, 129
    pouches, 142

tags, 143
    themed containers, 138
gilt-leaf candle pots, 49
gilt topiaries, 33
greenery
    cutting guide, 33
    decorations, 28-33
Grove Park Inn, 34

Icicle ornaments, 57
initial wreath, 128

Kitchen topiaries, 132

Mantels, 38
mantel scarf, napkin, 42
monogrammed
    napkins, 129
    ornaments, 127
    vase, 126
    wrapping paper, 129
    wreath, 128
moss and ribbon candleholders, 47

Napkins
    mantel scarf, 42
    monogrammed, 129
    rings, 56
natural gift wrap, 142
no-sew ornaments, 60
no-sew stocking, 60
no-sew tree skirt, 61
nutty topiaries, 132

Ornaments
    blackberry, 37
    icicle, 57
    monogrammed, 127
    no-sew, 60
    put-a-lid-on-it, 36
    ribbon, 130
ornament topiary, 43

Package toppers, 130, 142
paper gift bags, 142
party favors, peppermint, 65
peppermint
    candy dish, 63
    centerpiece, 62
    gift wraps, 142

package toppers, 142
party favors, 65
stack, 144
sticks, wrapped, 144
tree, 64
personalized
    napkins, 129
    ornaments, 127
    vase, 126
    wrapping paper, 129
    wreath, 128
pinecone candle rings, 46
pomanders, fruit, 53
potpourri pillows, 145

Ribbon
    bookmarks, 145
    ornaments, 130
    tree, 131
    wreath, 131

Silver-trimmed candles, 49
stockings, 60, 66

Tags, gift, 143
topiaries
    bay leaf, 133
    garlic globe, 133
    gilt, 33
    nutty, 132
    ornament, 43
    peppermint tree, 64
    ribbon, 131
tree
    decorating tips, 24, 36
    skirt, no-sew, 61
    topper, 36

Vase, monogrammed, 126
votive holders, 41, 45

Wrappings
    gift bags with beads, 141
    gift container, 140
    gift pouches, 142
    natural, 142
    package toppers, 130, 142
    paper, stamped, 129
wreaths, 12, 13, 39, 40, 54, 128, 131

RECIPE INDEX

Caramel-Nut
Pull-Apart
Bread

Almonds
Rice, Company, 18
Tartlets, Macaroon, 98
Ambrosia Trifle, 105
Appetizers
Crisps, Garlic-Pepper
Parmesan, 88
Dippers, BLT, 87
Pâté, Colorful Christmas, 87
Peppers, Crab-Stuffed, 88
Potato Wedges with Caviar,
Crisp, 88
Shrimp, Prosciutto-Wrapped, 88
Apple Filling, Golden, 135

Bacon
Dippers, BLT, 87
Beans
Chili, Fast-Break, 76
Green Bean Bundles, Lemon, 20
Green Beans with Orange-Shallot
Butter, French, 121
Salsa, Quick Fruited, 134
Beef, Ground
Chili, Fast-Break, 76
Lasagna, Slow Cooker, 76
Beef Tenderloin, Peppered, 115
Beets with Cloves and Port,
Glazed, 121
Beverages
Alcoholic
Bloody Marys, Overnight, 87
Sangría, Cranberry-
Raspberry, 87
Punch, Sparkling Cinnamon, 87
Biscotti, Pecan, 102
Biscuits, Chive 'n' Cheddar
Drop, 95
Breads. See also Biscuits, Muffins,
Pancakes, Rolls.
Breadsticks, Spicy Candy Cane, 95
Caramel-Nut Pull-Apart
Bread, 92
Cranberry Christmas Tree
Bread, 91
Eggnog Tea Bread, 95
Gingerbread, Lemon-Swirled, 95
Pesto Provolone Batter Bread, 94

Brownies, Double-Frosted
Bourbon, 103
Brownies, Peanutty Candy Bar, 105
Butter, French Green Beans with
Orange-Shallot, 121

Cakes. See also Cheesecakes.
Bûche de Noël, 109
Pound Cake, Chocolate
Chip, 105
Candy, Peanut Butter Crunch, 73
Caramel-Nut Pull-Apart Bread, 92
Casserole, Country Grits and
Sausage, 79
Caviar, Crisp Potato Wedges with, 88
Cheese. See also Cheesecakes.
Biscuits, Chive 'n' Cheddar
Drop, 95
Bread, Pesto Provolone Batter, 94
Casserole, Country Grits and
Sausage, 79
Crisps, Garlic-Pepper
Parmesan, 88
Frittata, Mediterranean, 78
Lasagna, Slow Cooker, 76
Muffins, Ham and Cheese, 91
Pasta with Creamy Alfredo
Sauce, 121
Pâté, Colorful Christmas, 87
Quiche, Chicken-Pecan, 79
Stuffing, Lemon-Parmesan, 118
Cheesecakes
Black-and-White
Cheesecake, 110
Café au Lait Cheesecake, 110
Cheesecake, Coconut, 110
Holly Cheesecake, 110

Orange Cheesecake, 110
Peppermint Cheesecake, 110
Raspberry Cheesecake, 110
Sampler, Cheesecake, 110
Walnut Cheesecake, 110
Cherries
Candied Cherries, 113
Sauce, Cherry, 117
Swirls, Chocolate-Cherry, 103
Chestnut Stuffing, Crown Roast of
Pork with, 116
Chicken
Dressing, Oyster, 75
Quiche, Chicken-Pecan, 79
Ragoût, Fruited Chicken, 76
Chili, Fast-Break, 76
Chocolate
Bûche de Noël, 109
Buttercream, Rich
Chocolate, 109
Cake, Chocolate Chip
Pound, 105
Candy, Peanut Butter Crunch, 73
Cheesecake, Black-and-
White, 110
Cookies
Brownies, Double-Frosted
Bourbon, 103
Brownies, Peanutty Candy
Bar, 105
Chip Cookies, Aunt Gladys'
Chocolate, 71
Kissy Cookies, 99
Swirls, Chocolate-Cherry, 103
Swirls, Chocolate-Orange, 103
Ultimate Chocolate Comfort
Cookies, 98

Chocolate (*continued*)

Dessert Squares, Mocha, 105
Glaze, Chocolate, 103
Ice Cream Bowls, Toffee
    Crunch, 107
Muffins, Hot Chocolate, 91
Muffins, White Chocolate-
    Macadamia Nut, 91
Coconut Cheesecake, 110
Cookies
Biscotti, Pecan, 102
Brownies, Double-Frosted
    Bourbon, 103
Brownies, Peanutty Candy
    Bar, 105
Canes, Peppermint Cookie, 102
Drop
    Chocolate Chip Cookies, Aunt
        Gladys', 71
    Chocolate Comfort Cookies,
        Ultimate, 98
    Lizzies, Oatmeal-Fruitcake, 98
Refrigerator
    Gingerbread Men, 101
    Shortbread, Rosemary, 101
    Swirls, Chocolate-Cherry, 103
    Swirls, Chocolate-Orange, 103
Kissy Cookies, 99
Peanut Butter Cookies,
    Chunky, 99
Peanut Butter Fingers, 99
Springerle, 101
Sugar Cookies, Melt-in-Your-
    Mouth Iced, 97
Cornbread, Sage and Onion, 93
Cornbread, Skillet, 75
Crab-Stuffed Peppers, 88
Cranberries
Bread, Cranberry Christmas
    Tree, 91
Cookies, Ultimate Chocolate
    Comfort, 98
Salad, Cranberry-Pear, 85
Sangría, Cranberry-Raspberry, 87
Sauce, Sweet Potatoes with
    Cranberry, 18
Custard, Boiled, 72
Custards with Candied Cherries,
    Eggnog, 112

Date Pudding, Upside-Down, 106
Desserts. *See also* Cakes, Cheesecakes,
    Cookies, Custard, Pies and
    Pastries, Pudding.
Candy, Peanut Butter Crunch, 73
Cherries, Candied, 113
Crisp, Winter Fruit, 135
Elephant Ears, 107
Ice Cream Bowls, Toffee
    Crunch, 107
Mocha Dessert Squares, 105
Sauce, Maple, 111
Sauce, Praline, 21
Trifle, Ambrosia, 105
Dressing. *See also* Stuffings.
Oyster Dressing, 75
Duck with Cherry Sauce, Roast, 117

Eggnog Custards with Candied
    Cherries, 112
Eggnog Tea Bread, 95
Eggs. *See also* Quiche.
Casserole, Country Grits and
    Sausage, 79
Frittata, Mediterranean, 78

Frittata, Mediterranean, 78
Frostings, Fillings, and Toppings
Apple Filling, Golden, 135
Berry Filling, Mixed, 135
Chocolate Buttercream,
    Rich, 109
Chocolate Glaze, 103
Honey, Georgia Peach, 136

Icing, Royal, 97
Oatmeal-Walnut Crumble
    Topping, 135
White Frosting, 103
Fruit. *See also* specific types.
Crisp, Winter Fruit, 135
Filling, Mixed Berry, 135
Lizzies, Oatmeal-Fruitcake, 98
Ragoût, Fruited Chicken, 76
Salad, Stained Glass, 20
Salsa, Quick Fruited, 134
Syrup, Lemon-Berry, 136

Game. *See* Duck, Quail.
Greens, Wilted Winter, 121
Grits and Sausage Casserole,
    Country, 79

Ham. *See also* Bacon, Pork.
Baked Ham, Tawny, 115
Country Ham, Black-Eyed Peas
    with Caramelized Onion
    and, 122
Muffins, Ham and Cheese, 91
Pasta with Creamy Alfredo
    Sauce, 121
Honey, Georgia Peach, 136

Ice Cream Bowls, Toffee Crunch, 107

Lasagna, Slow Cooker, 76
Lemon
Curls, Lemon, 119
Gingerbread, Lemon-Swirled, 95

**Toffee Crunch
Ice Cream Bowl**

Green Bean Bundles, Lemon, 20
Springerle, Lemon, 101
Stuffing, Lemon-Parmesan, 118
Syrup, Lemon-Berry, 136
Turkey, Lemon-Sage, 118

Maple Sauce, 111
Meringue Mushrooms, 109
Mix, Hearty Cornmeal Pancake, 136
Molasses Muffins, Pumpkin-, 92
Muffins
    Chocolate-Macadamia Nut
        Muffins, White, 91
    Chocolate Muffins, Hot, 91
    Ham and Cheese Muffins, 91
    Pumpkin-Molasses Muffins, 92
Mushrooms
    Lasagna, Slow Cooker, 76
    Rice, Company, 18

Oatmeal-Fruitcake Lizzies, 98
Oatmeal-Walnut Crumble
        Topping, 135
Olives
    Frittata, Mediterranean, 78
Onions
    Caramelized Onion and Country
        Ham, Black-eyed Peas
        with, 122
    Cornbread, Sage and Onion, 93
    Glazed Onions, 19
Oranges
    Ambrosia Trifle, 105
    Butter, French Green Beans with
        Orange-Shallot, 121
    Cheesecake, Orange, 110
    Swirls, Chocolate-Orange, 103
Oyster Dressing, 75

Pancakes
    Good Morning Pancakes, 136
    Mix, Hearty Cornmeal
        Pancake, 136
Pastas. See also Lasagna.
    Alfredo Sauce, Pasta with
        Creamy, 121
    Thai Pasta with Turkey, 79
Pâté, Colorful Christmas, 87
Peach Dish, Easy, 122
Peach Honey, Georgia, 136

Peanut Butter
    Brownies, Peanutty Candy
        Bar, 105
    Candy, Peanut Butter Crunch, 73
    Cookies, Chunky Peanut
        Butter, 99
    Pasta with Turkey, Thai, 79
Pears
    Gingered Pears in Acorn
        Squash, 123
    Salad, Cranberry-Pear, 85
Peas with Caramelized Onion
        and Country Ham,
        Black-Eyed, 122
Pecans
    Biscotti, Pecan, 102
    Cookies, Aunt Gladys' Chocolate
        Chip, 71
    Cookies, Ultimate Chocolate
        Comfort, 98
    Quiche, Chicken-Pecan, 79
Peppermint Cheesecake, 110
Peppermint Cookie Canes, 102
Peppers, Crab-Stuffed, 88
Pesto Provolone Batter Bread, 94
Pies and Pastries
    Pumpkin Chess Pie, 21
    Tartlets, Macaroon, 98
Pork with Chestnut Stuffing,
        Crown Roast of, 116
Potatoes. See also Sweet Potatoes.
    Wedges with Caviar, Crisp
        Potato, 88
Praline
    Praline Sauce, 21
    Syrup, Praline Crunch, 136
Prosciutto-Wrapped Shrimp, 88
Pudding, Upside-Down
        Date, 106
Pudding with Maple Sauce, Spiced
        Steamed, 111
Pumpkin
    Muffins, Pumpkin-
        Molasses, 92
    Pie, Pumpkin Chess, 21
    Pudding with Maple Sauce,
        Spiced Steamed, 111

Quail, Nannie's Smothered, 70
Quiche, Chicken-Pecan, 79

Ragoût, Fruited Chicken, 76
Raspberry Cheesecake, 110
Raspberry Sangría, Cranberry-, 87
Rice, Company, 18
Rolls, Herbed Fan Tan Dinner, 92
Rosemary Shortbread, 101

Salads
    Asian Salad, 79
    Cranberry-Pear Salad, 85
    Stained Glass Salad, 20
Salsa, Quick Fruited, 134
Sauces. See also Honey, Salsa, Syrup.
    Cherry Sauce, 117
    Maple Sauce, 111
    Praline Sauce, 21
Sausage Casserole, Country Grits
        and, 79
Seafood. See Crab, Oysters, Shrimp.
Shrimp, Prosciutto-Wrapped, 88
Slow Cooker Lasagna, 76
Squash, Gingered Pears in
        Acorn, 123
Stuffings. See also Dressing.
    Chestnut Stuffing, Crown Roast
        of Pork with, 116
    Lemon-Parmesan Stuffing, 118
Sweet Potatoes with Cranberry
        Sauce, 18
Syrup, Lemon-Berry, 136
Syrup, Praline Crunch, 136

Tomatoes
    Bloody Marys, Overnight, 87
    Dippers, BLT, 87
    Pâté, Colorful Christmas, 87
Trifle, Ambrosia, 105
Turkey, Lemon-Sage, 118
Turkey, Thai Pasta with, 79

Vegetables. See specific types.

Walnuts
    Bread, Caramel-Nut
        Pull-Apart, 92
    Cheesecake, Walnut, 110
    Pudding, Upside-Down Date, 106
    Salad, Cranberry-Pear, 85
    Topping, Oatmeal-Walnut
        Crumble, 135

CONTRIBUTORS

Editorial Contributors

Jean Allsopp (photography)

Van Chaplin (photography)

Melanie Clarke

Cheryl S. Dalton (photography)

Susan Dosier (contributing editor)

Colleen Duffley (photography)

Connie Formby

Jan Gautro

Susan Hancock/Elfin Glitz

Margot Hotchkiss

Sylvia Martin (photography)

Connie Matricardi

Duffy Morrison

Joetta Moulden (contributing editor)

Cecile Y. Nierodzinski

Dondra G. Parham

Catherine Pewitt

Susan Ray

Meg Rice/Elfin Glitz

Charles Walton IV (photography)

Mindy Wilson (contributing writer)

Recipe Contributors

Margaret Agnew

Jackie Bergenheier

Karen Celentano

Liz Cingel

Kay Y. Dale

Christine Hardwick

Carolyn Hollingsworth

Margie Klaeppel

Elizabeth Luckett

James O. Michelinie

Debby Maugans Nakos

Jean Scott

Elizabeth Taliaferro

Alan Wysong

Thanks to the following homeowners:

Sybil Duncan

Judy and Rusty Fuller

Jennie and Tom Hale

Carolyn and John Hartman

Alyce and James Head

Suzanne and Alan Pizzitola

Faye and Vince Shannon

My favorite holiday recipe:

_____

_____

_____

Traditions we started this year:

The peaceful moment: